IT時代の オールラウンド ビジネス英語

早稲田大学教授
篠田義明 著

Business Communication for All Purposes in the IT Age

南雲堂

**Business Communication
for All Purposes in the IT Age**

by

Yoshiaki Shinoda

©2001 All rights reserved.

No part of this book may be reproduced, in any form or by any means, without permission in writing from the author.

はじめに

　本書は，英語を使ってビジネスやそれにまつわるコミュニケーションをはかる際に頻出する手紙やその他のドキュメントの豊富な例文をあげて，詳しい解説を付けたものである。ほとんどが実例なので実務の場で直接利用できるであろう。大学，高等学校上級，企業内研修，商業英語検定試験 (日本商工会議所主催) の準備，TEP Test (早稲田大学・ミシガン大学実用ライティング英語検定試験) の準備にも利用できるようにした。

　国際化の渦潮に呑まれている今の日本は，方策を立てずに脱出しようともがけば沈没の憂き目にさらされるであろう。このような苦境の中で取るべき道は，今や地球語とまでいわれている英語という櫓を上手に漕ぐしか策はあるまい。本書ではその策を詳述した。日本の企業は，原料の輸入と製造加工品の輸出という従来の貿易取引の中にだけ止まっておれなくなり，現地生産，海外直接投資のような様々な形態へと進んでいる。このように，企業の国際化と多国籍化が進むと企業間だけでなく，企業内による英語によるコミュニケーションも避けられない。

　国際化は様々な形態でわれわれに忍び寄ってきている。三国間取引が出現したり，プラント輸出の代金をその国の商品を輸入することで相殺するという Counter Purchase という取引も現れている。しかし，実情はどうであれ，われわれは地球語である英語を使ってビジネスをしなければならない現状にいるといえよう。

　ビジネスの英語で，特に大切で日本人に弱いと思える事項を第1章に「ビジネス英語の特長」としてまとめた。ここを参考にすると今まで曖昧模糊の状態で使っていた，日本人に弱い英語の一端が自信を持って使えるようになるものと確信する。第2章では手紙の構成，第3章から第12章まででは各種ビジネスレターの特質と実例，第13章では各種文書，特にファクシミリと，E-mail, Short Business Reports,

議事録，ネゴシエーション，プレゼンテーション，推薦状，履歴書，冠婚葬祭の英語の特質と例文をそれぞれ紹介した。また，参考として，世界の貨幣単位，各国の日付の書き方の相違，国際電話番号も紹介したのでお役に立つものと確信する。

　本著を執筆にあたり，まず鳥谷剛三先生と伊東克己先生から受けた多年のご高庇を特記しなければならない。紋切り型のようだが鳥谷先生にお目にかからなければ本書は生まれなかったであろう。貿易実務・慣行については中村那詮先生に，その一部の校正までお手を煩わせ，貴重なアドバイスをいただいた。編集に当たっては南雲堂の青木泰祐氏から終始暖かい激励をたまわった。各位に衷心より感謝しなければならない。

　最後に，広範なため不測の思い違いや誤りや強引なところがあろうかと思う。ご利用者の厳しいご叱正をたまわりたい。

２００１年１月

篠田　義明

本書の構成と利用法

● **構成**
　第１章では，英語でビジネスする際に日本人が特に注意をした方がよいと思える「ビジネス英語の特長」を説明した。
　第２章では，企業でよく質問を受ける「ビジネスレターの構成」について，ほとんどの質問に答えられるように詳述した。
　第３章から第12章までは，日本の企業で頻出する英文手紙の実例を示し，詳注を施した。
　第13章では，現在のビジネスでは避けられないファクシミリの英語と E-mail の英語で注意すべき点を述べ，例文を示した。

● **利用法**
　第１章から読み始めてもよいし，第２章から始めてもよいし，第３章から始めてもよい。第３章から始めた場合は，第１章と第２章は，是非，読んでほしい。
　なお，例文の年号のなかで，20XXとしたのは，XXに各自で１桁，２桁目に数字を自由に入れて読んで欲しいとの意図からである。

目　次

はじめに 3
本書の構成と利用法 4

第1章　ビジネス英語の特長 11
1.1　大切な語調 12
1.2　Softener が大切 13
1.3　一語一義に徹する 16
　　1.3.1　動詞 16
　　1.3.2　名詞 17
　　1.3.3　形容詞 18
　　1.3.4　副詞 18
1.4　打消しよりも肯定で 19
1.5　受動態と能動態を使い分ける 21
1.6　不要な関係代名詞は使わない 23
1.7　however, therefore のような接続詞の句読法に注意 ... 24
1.8　注意すべき助動詞 26
1.9　差別語を避ける 29
1.10　Subject の書き方 31
1.11　パラグラフのまとめ方 32

第2章　ビジネスレターの構成
2.1　レターペーパー 33
2.2　構成要素 34
　　2.2.1　必携項目 34
　　2.2.2　任意項目 49
2.3　様式 54
2.4　句読法 57

2. 5　封筒 58
　　2. 5. 1　Mail Direction 58
　　2. 5. 2　折り方 59

第3章　取引申込み
3. 1　引合い（1） 61
　　3. 1. 1　内容構成 61
　　3. 1. 2　例文 62
3. 2　引合い（2） 66
　　3. 2. 1　内容構成 66
　　3. 2. 2　例文 67

第4章　取引申込みの返事
4. 1　内容構成 70
4. 2　例文 71

第5章　オファー
5. 1　種類と英文の特長 77
5. 2　例文 79

第6章　オファーへの返事
6. 1　種類とその対処法 83
6. 2　例文 84

第7章　代理店
7. 1　種類 86
7. 2　Agent と Distributor 86
7. 3　例文 87

第8章　注文とその返事
8. 1　記載事項 95
8. 2　例文 95

第9章　遅延状

   9.1　参考覚書 100
   9.2　内容構成 100
   9.3　例文 101

第10章　積出し

   10.1　船積書類 104
   10.2　船荷書類 105
   10.3　船荷証券 105
   10.4　海上保険 105
   10.5　航空貨物保険 106
   10.6　貿易条件 106
   10.7　例文 107

第11章　支払い

   11.1　手形の種類 111
   11.2　支払い時期 111
   11.3　信用状の種類 112
   11.4　簡単な取立状 113
   11.5　例文 114

第12章　クレーム

   12.1　発生するケース 120
   12.2　対処法 121
   12.3　内容構成 121
      12.3.1　苦情の手紙 121
      12.3.2　苦情への返事 121
   12.4　例文 122

第13章　各種英文書

- 13.1　開店披露状 125
- 13.2　お礼状 127
- 13.3　ファクシミリの英語 133
  - 13.3.1　カバーシートの例 133
  - 13.3.2　通信文の例 135
- 13.4　E-mailの英語 138
  - 13.4.1　基本形式 138
  - 13.4.2　英語の特長 138
  - 13.4.3　多用される略語 141
  - 13.4.4　スマイリー記号 142
  - 13.4.5　例文 143
- 13.5　Short Business Reports 145
  - 13.5.1　種類 145
  - 13.5.2　内容構成 145
  - 13.5.3　Heading 146
  - 13.5.4　Body of the Reports 147
  - 13.5.5　例文 149
- 13.6　議事録 151
  - 13.6.1　記載事項 152
  - 13.6.2　記録者の注意点 152
  - 13.6.3　会議についての諸注意 152
  - 13.6.4　議題、協議事項、議事の書き方 153
  - 13.6.5　構成要素と実例 154
- 13.7　English in Negotiation 161
  - 13.7.1　相手を非難する英語 161
  - 13.7.2　心に留めておくべき点 162
  - 13.7.3　避けるべき態度 163
  - 13.7.4　避けるべき英語 163

- 13.7.5 好感[悪印象]を与える英語 166
- 13.7.6 同意を求める表現 166
- 13.7.7 同意する表現 167
- 13.7.8 反対意見の表現 167
- 13.7.9 相手が憤慨しているか否かを聞く表現 168
- 13.7.10 怒りを押えるように依頼する表現 168
- 13.7.11 注意すべき表現 168
- 13.7.12 適切な反応表現 170
- 13.8 English in Presentation 171
  - 13.8.1 挨拶 171
  - 13.8.2 製品・アイデアの説明 171
  - 13.8.3 特長の説明 171
  - 13.8.4 説明の終了 172
  - 13.8.5 質問に答える 172
  - 13.8.6 終了 173
- 13.9 人物紹介状と推薦状 174
  - 13.9.1 人物紹介状 174
    - 13.9.1.1 書出しの例 174
    - 13.9.1.2 例文 175
  - 13.9.2 推薦状 177
    - 13.9.2.1 例文 177
- 13.10 英文履歴書 182
  - 13.10.1 自分を売込む例 183
  - 13.10.2 履歴書の例 185
- 13.11 冠婚葬祭の英語 186
  - 13.11.1 注意事項 186
  - 13.11.2 お悔やみ状 189
  - 13.11.3 Chrismas Card 190
  - 13.11.4 Valelntine Day 194

14章　参考

　14．1　世界各国の貨幣単位 195
　14．2　各国の数字による日付表示表 200
　14．3　各国の国際電話番号 201

和文索引　　 203
英文索引　　 212

第1章

ビジネス英語の特長

　英語を使って国際社会で仕事をする人は，英語だけの知識では通用しない。実務・慣習の知識，風俗習慣の相違，ビジネスに適する英語を身に付けて「真剣勝負」でかからないと誰からも信用されないで，ひとり取り残されてしまう。

　実務の基本はそれぞれの箇所で簡単に触れた。詳しくは貿易実務の専門書で研究されたい。風俗習慣については，本書でも触れた。しかし外形的な面以外に価値観の相違，信仰・考え方の相違などもあり，実に範囲も広い。国により異なるので，取引をする相手国の民族の研究も必携である。

　ファクシミリや E-mail を使ってコミュニケーションをする企業も増えている。ファクシミリでは略式を好み，E-mail は略式を好むと同時に会話体に近い英語を使う。しかし，コミュニケーションに利用するシステムは違っても，そこを貫く英語は同じである。

　昔からビジネスレターを作成する要件として頭が C で始まる単語を並べて，これを鉄則としている。Clearness (Clarity 明快), Conciseness (簡潔), Consideration (配慮), Correctness (正確), Concreteness (具体性)である。これに Courtesy (丁重), Completeness (完結) を加えて 7 C's を唱えている人もいる。更に，多少の論理性を考えて，Clear, Candid (公平な), Concise, Correct, Coherent (筋の通った), Complete, Concrete, Convincing (説得力のある), Constructive (建設的な), Conversational (会話体で) の10C'sを勧めている参考書もある。

　いずれにしても，自分本位に走らず，相手の立場に立ち，常に相手を尊重する気持ちで明確・正確・簡潔な英文作成にあたることを忘れてはならない。

　次に，日本人が英文でビジネスレターを書くときに特に注意したほうがよいと思える点を10C'sの考え方から説明する。

1.1　大切な語調

　日本語にも，尊敬語，丁寧語，謙譲語とあるように，英語にもこれにあたる表現がある。状況に応じて適切な語調 (Tone) で表現することはビジネスレターのみならず，ファクシミリや E-mail のような「紙上やディスプレイ上の会話」でも大切である。日本語の手紙でも，正しい敬語を使わないと受信者は発信者を軽蔑するだけでなく，協力する意志を失い，一緒に仕事をする気にならないだろう。あなたの書いた一本の手紙が会社を代表していることを忘れてはならない。

　いろいろなケースが考えられるが，ここではごく基本的なスタイルについて述べる。

＊「〜を注文<u>いたします</u>」に

  1)　We *want to* place an order for 〜

  2)　We *would like to* place an order for 〜

  3)　We *are glad to* place an order for 〜

  4)　We *are pleased to* place an order for 〜

  5)　We *have the pleasure of* placing an order for 〜

  6)　It *is our great pleasure to* place an order for 〜

などの表現があり，相手に与える印象は異なる。どれを使うかは，状況にもよるが，1)は本当に注文したい気持ちが出ている。2)は消極的である。3)は口語調である。4)は多用される。5)はやや格式張った表現である。6)は格式張り過ぎていて，標準英語とはいえず，このような場合には使えない。

＊「〜をお知らせ<u>ください</u>」に

  1)　*Tell* us 〜

  2)　*Please tell* us 〜

  3)　*Please let us know* 〜

  4)　We *wish to know* 〜

  5)　We *will (would) be glad to know* 〜

  6)　We *shall be obliged if you will (would) let us know* 〜

7) *Please favor us with* ～
8) *We'd appreciate it if you could let us know* ～

などがあるが，1)はあまりにもぶっきらぼうだから失礼，2), 3)は丁寧に本当に知らせてほしいという積極的な気持ちが込められている。5)は口語調だから書く英語ではあまり用いられない。6)は旧式，7), 8)はへりくだり過ぎるので，通常は使わない。

問合わせたり，尋ねたりするときも，We wish to know if ～. とか，We would like to know if ～. がソフトでよい。次の「1.2 Softener が大切」の項も参照のこと。

1.2 Softenerが大切

突飛で，失礼なスタイルの手紙は相手を不愉快にさせる。そのため，相手は協力してくれず，ビジネスも不成功に終わる羽目に陥る。

① 「ご要求の商品は明日小包で空輸します」

Negative: The merchandise you requested will be shipped tomorrow by airfreight.

この文は無味乾燥である。そこでsoftenerを付ける。

Positive: *We are happy to let you know* that the merchandise you requested will be shipped ～.

イタリックのsoftenerを加えると英文が丁寧になる。

② 「修理のためにあなたが当社に送られた携帯電話の保証期間は切れております」

Negative: The warranty has expired on the cellular phone you sent us for repair.

この文はお客を無視している。そこで，次の文のようにイタリックの部分を加えると丁寧になる。

Positive: *We regret to have to tell you that* the warranty has expired on the cellular phone you sent us ～.

③「ご要求の船外エンジンが未着とのことですね」

Negative: You have not received the outboard engines you wanted.
この文では，未着に対して遺憾の気持ちがでていない。

Positive: *I am very sorry that* you have not received the outboard 〜.
のようにイタリックの softener を加えるとソフトになる。しかし，I am sorry 〜 は責任をとることも意味するので無闇に使ってはならない。

Softener の考えは会話にも応用するとよい。
たとえば，「お金を貸してくれ」と懇願されて「お貸しいたしましょう」に
 "I'll lend you some." よりは
 "I'll *be glad to* lend you some."
とイタリックの部分を加えると相手を尊敬した柔らかい英語になる。

「巧く」いくようなときは，be delighted to; be glad to; be happy to; be pleased to などを用い，「失敗する」ようなときは，be afraid; regret; be sorry などを用いる。前の「**大切な語調**」の項も参照のこと。

次の例文で **Negative** と **Positive** の英語との tone の違いに注意しよう。

④「再考慮いたします」

Negative: We will reconsider it.

Positive: *We will be delighted to* reconsider it.

⑤「オファーをお送りいたします」

Negative: We will send you our offer.

Positive: *We will be pleased to* send you our offer.

⑥「ご要求通り当社の最新のカタログを同封いたします」

Negative: We will enclose our recent catalog as you requested.

Positive: *We are pleased to* enclose our recent catalog as you requested.

⑦「製品は明日の午後あなたのところにお届けいたします」

Negative: I will bring the product to your place tomorrow afternoon.

Positive: *I will be happy to* bring the product to 〜.

⑧「貴社の委託番号について苦情を申さなければなりません」

Negative: We will have to complain about your consignment number.

Positive: *We regret to* have to complain about 〜.

⑨「先約がありますので，この機会は諦めます」

Negative: I will have to turn down the opportunity because of other commitments.

Positive: *I'm afraid that* I will have to turn down 〜.

⑩「貴殿のプリンターは保証期限が過ぎております」

Negative: The warranty has expired on your printer.

Positive: *We are sorry, but* the warranty has expired on 〜.

⑪「学校は4月初めに始まりますので，3月25日までに小冊子をどうしても私に送ってください」

Negative: Since our class begins in early April, you must send us the booklets without fail by March 25.

Positive: Since our class begins in early April, *we would be more than happy if you could* send us the booklets by March 25.

　　　　　[Negative の文で you must では要求が強すぎる]

⑫「当社は食品廃棄物処理機などの幅広い商品を扱う老舗の輸入業者です」

Negative: We introduce ourselves as established importers of a wide variety of commodities, including Food Waste Disposers.

Positive: *We wish to* introduce ourselves as 〜.

1.3　一語一義に徹する

一つの単語が一つだけの明確な意味を伝えないと，書き手と読み手の考えが異なり，結果も違ってくる。ビジネスレターでは一つしか意味を持たない単語を使用するよう常に心掛けねばならない。これは，動詞，名詞，形容詞，副詞などのすべての語(句)に適用できる。

1.3.1　動詞

(1) **Negative:** Please *send* to us by the end of May the parts we ordered.
（ご注文の部品は5月末までにお送りください）
[ここでは send が曖昧]

Positive Please *airmail* to us by the end of 〜.

(2) **Negative:** The best way for you is to *choose* our brand.
（最善の方法は当社のブランドをお選びになることです）
[choose が曖昧]

Positive: The best way for you is to *buy* our brand.

(3) **Negative:** Don't *use* the clock in the sun.
（時計は日向で使わないでください）
[use が曖昧]

Positive: Don't *install* the clock 〜.

(4) **Negative:** Please *tell* us your lowest possible prices.
（貴社の最低値段をお知らせください）
[tell が曖昧]

Positive: Please *quote* us your lowest possible prices.

(5) **Negative:** The material was *damaged* by the heavy *rain*.
（その材料は大雨で被害を受けた）
[damage も heavy rain も曖昧]

Positive: The material was *discolored* in *torrents*.

(6) **Negative:** When *you send* us your check, we will begin work.
[send が曖昧]

Positive: When *we receive* your check (*or* Upon receipt of your check), we will 〜.
[受領して始めて信用できる]

1.3.2 名詞

「メーカー」に対して maker だけだと思ってはならない。manufacturer もある。メーカーは個人を指すが manufacturer は企業を指す,と説明している辞書もある。

Something is wrong with my watch; I'm sending it back to the *manufacturer.* (時計が故障したので,メーカーへ送り返すところだ) では大袈裟な感じがする。この場合 manufacturer は maker が適切だろう。

The printer does not work, so we will send it back to the *maker.* (格式張った手紙で相手を指すときは maker よりは manufacturer が無難といえる。

「生産者」なら producer である。The country I visited is one of the world's leading oil *producers.* (私が訪問した国は世界で主要なオイル産出国です)

「自動車」を car とか automobile, motorcar では,どんな「車」か曖昧なので車種やモデルを明記しないと相手には分からない。

「道路」も road だけではない。alley; avenue; boulevard; expressway; highway, lane; line; motorway; pass; path; roadway; route; street; thoroughfare; toll road; track などがあるので,違いがわからなければ辞書で確認してから使うべきである。これらの違いを知るには類語辞典か *Thesaurus* がよい。

(1) **Negative:** The wall was *damaged* by the *rain*.
[damage と rain が曖昧]
Positive: The wall *collapsed* in the *storm*.

(2) **Negative:** The bus I took ran along the *alley*.

[バスは alley（小道）を走れない]

Positive: The bus I took ran along the highway.

1.3.3　形容詞

曖昧な形容詞を使うと，受信者は発信者がいい加減な文を書いていると解して，発信者を信用しなくなる。

(1) **Negative:** Mr. Suzuki is a *nice* supervisor.
[nice は曖昧]

Positive: Mr. Suzuki is a *considerate* (or *well-liked; well-respected*) supervisor.

(2) **Negative:** He has published the *awful* records of the meeting.
[awful では「ひどい」で曖昧]

Positive: He has published the *inconsistent* (or *embarrassing*) records of ～.

1.3.4　副詞

副詞は場合によっては曖昧になるから注意して使おう。

(1) **Negative:** Please let us know your answer *soon*.　[soon が曖昧]

Positive: Please let us know your answer before *February 2*.

(2) **Negative:** Your investment should increase *significantly* next year.　[significantly が曖昧]

Positive: Your investment should increase *by 10 percent* next year.

(3) **Negative:** Please send us your check *as soon as possible*.
[as soon as possible が曖昧]

Positive: Please send us your check *by the end of May*.
[期日を指定する]

(4) **Negative:** Please let us know if our Order No. 234 *is available for prompt shipment*.　[*is* 以下が曖昧]

Positive: Please let us know if our Order No. 234 can be shipped *at the end of May*.

1.4　打消しよりも肯定で

日本人は打消しが好きである。

「真珠湾を忘れるな」は英語の原文は Remember Pearl Harbor. である。「このドアから入ってはいけません」は Don't enter ～ではなく，Use another door. [Use the other door. ともいう] が普通である。

no less than ten の代わりに at least ten; ten or more; a minimum of ten が好ましいし，no more than ten よりも ten at the most; a maximum of ten が好ましい。また, neglect; you claim; fail to; your complaint のような相手にマイナスのイメージを与える語 (句) の使用も控えたい。

相手の要求に対して，"No." と一方的に答えたのでは相手の気分を害してしてしまう。"No." 一語でビジネスも終わりにならないとも限らない。ビジネスの世界では，たとえ "No." であっても相手の気分を害さず，しかも自社にプラスになるような代案を示す心構えを忘れてはならない。また，相手にマイナスのイメージを与える語の使用も慎みたい。

(1) **Negative:** I will *not* write you until I finish the research.
（その調査が終わるまではお手紙を書きません）

　Positive: I will write you as soon as I finish ～.
（その調査が終わり次第お手紙いたします）

(2) **Negative:** You *claim* that we did *not* enclose all the parts you requested.
（ご要求の部品すべてを当社が同封しなかったと貴殿はおっしゃられます）

　Positive: We regret any delays in your production caused by the missing parts you requested.
（ご要求の部品がなかったため貴社の生産が遅れたとの

こと申し訳ございません）

(3) **Negative:** In your July 10 order, *you neglected* to specify the model of the machine you require.

（7月10日の貴殿のご注文で，貴殿はご要求の機械のモデル名を明記なさいませんでした）

Positive: Thank you for your July 10 order. Just let me know the model of the machine you prefer, and I'll airmail it at once.

（7月10日付けご注文有難うございました。ご希望の機械のモデル名をお知らせください。すぐ空輸いたします）

(4) **Negative:** Your June 15 *complaint* letter has been received.

（6月15日付けの苦情のお手紙受取りました）

Positive: Thank you for the friendly suggestion made in your June 15 letter.

（6月15日付け貴信でお寄せくださいましたご厚意あふれるご提案に厚く御礼申し上げます）

(5) **Negative:** We are out of stock of the model you ordered, so we *cannot* send it to you at once.

（ご注文のモデルは現在在庫がございませんので直ぐにはお送り致しかねます）

Positive: The model you ordered is extremely popular, and we quickly sold all we had in stock. However, we've placed a rush order for more and are promised delivery within one week. You may expect delivery within ten days.

（ご注文のモデルは極めて人気があるため手持ちが直ぐ売切れました。至急注文いたしました。当方へ一週間以内に納品してくださる確約を取りましたので，貴殿

へは10日以内に納品できると思います）

[「10日以内に納品できる」と納品日を明記することが大切]

1.5 受動態と能動態を使い分ける

受動態は動作主が曖昧になるので使わない方がよいと注意している参考書があるが，受動態を使うのは，それなりの理由があるからで，正しく使い分けると効果が出る。しかし，文法ミスを避けようとして，故意に受動態を使ってはならない。

You did not enclose the check. (あなたは小切手を同封しませんでした) では，相手を責めている。そこで，受動態で The check was not enclosed. とすると You が引っ込むので，失礼さが解消される。

(1) **Negative:** Regular orders *are expected* to be placed for these products.

（この製品は定期的にご注文されます）

[誰が注文するか不明]

Positive: *We expect* to place regular orders for these products.

[注文者が明確]

(2) **Negative:** The remaining items *are needed* urgently.

（残りの品目は至急必要とされています）

[必要としている人が不明確]

Positive: *We need* the remaining items urgently.

[必要としている人が明確]

(3) **Negative:** *It was felt that* the expenses were too great.

（支出は多すぎると思われました）

[動作主が不明確]

Positive: *We felt* the expenses were too great.

[動作主が明確] しかし，行為者を隠したい場合は受動態を使う。

(4) **Negative:** *It was discovered that*, of the total 20 cases, one case contained the material whose quality was much inferior to that of the sample submitted.

（全20ケースのうち，1ケースには送られてまいりましたサンプルよりはるかに劣っている材料が入っていることが分かりました）

[動作主が不明確]

Positive: *We discovered that* ～.

[動作主を明確にして，かつ相手に強く申し出たい場合に動作主を主語にする]

(5) **Negative:** *You have made* two errors in the minutes.

（あなたは，議事録で二つの間違いをしています）

[相手を直接責めているので失礼]

Positive: Two errors *were found* in the minutes.

受動態の効果的な用法も忘れてはならない。次のように，相手に行為者を伝える必要がないときは受動態を用いる。

Positive: Our company *was founded* in 1933.

（当社は1933年に創設されました）

Positive: The goods *were unpacked* yesterday.

（荷物は昨日開けられました）

Positive: Your business and credit standing will *be checked* on May 30.

（貴社の営業状態と信用状態の調査は5月30日に行われます）

[We will check ... とか I will check ... で始めると「当社が」「私が」調べることを正面に打ち出すことになる]

1.6 不要な関係代名詞は使わない

　文法上の誤りを恐れてか，あるいは日本語に影響されてか，日本人は関係代名詞を好んで用いる傾向がある。I met a girl who is beautiful. のような英文は I met a beautiful girl. の方が自然である。無意味な関係代名詞は，いたずらに文を長くし，読み難くするのでその使用を注意すべきである。

(1) **Negative:** I am sending you a check *which* amounts to $1,000.
　　　　　　（総額1,000ドルの小切手をお送りいたします）
　Positive: I am sending you a check *for* $1,000.
　　　　　　[a $1,000 check. でもよい]

(2) **Negative:** Mr. Suzuki is a very good technician, *who* works efficiently and imaginatively.
　　　　　　（鈴木氏は非常によい技術者で，有能で想像力豊かな仕事をする）　　　　　　― TEP Test 18回
　　　　　　[good が曖昧だが関係代名詞以下で説明しているので削除]
　Positive: Mr. Suzuki is an efficient and imaginative technician.

(3) **Negative:** The consultant, *who* came from the Heian Corporation, gave a speech *that* was boring.
　　　　　　（平安会社から来たコンサルタントの挨拶は退屈だった）
　Positive: The Heian Corporation consultant gave a boring speech.
　　　　　　[派遣を強く意味したければ The consultant from the Heian Corporation ～. とする]

(4) **Negative:** The report, *which* consists of three volumes, outlined the full responsibilities *that* each manager has to assume.
　　　　　　（3巻からなる報告書にはそれぞれのマネージャーが負わなければならない全責任の要点が書いてあった）

Positive: The three-volume report outlined the full responsibilities of each manager.

(5) **Negative:** The System Engineering Division, *which* is one of Heian's four divisions, is operated by two ultra-modern plants, *which* are the Meiji Plant and the Showa Plant.

（平安社の四つの部門の一つであるシステム工学部門は明治工場と昭和工場という二つの超近代的な工場で運営されている）

Positive: The System Engineering Division, one of Heian's four divisions, is operated by two ultra-modern plants: the Meiji Plant and the Showa Plant.

1.7　howeverやthereforeのような接続詞の句読法に注意

表記の類の接続詞とそこに用いる句読点との誤用が目立つ。

(1)「注文が急に増えていますので在庫が減っています」

Negative: Orders are increasing rapidly, *therefore*, our stock is decreasing. これでは，*Therefore* orders are increasing rapidly, our stock is decreasing. と同じことになり，orders are 〜 rapidly, の文と our stock is decreasing の文がつながらない。つまり「したがって，注文が急に増えた」になる。ここでの therefore は，あくまでも「したがって，在庫が減っている」のことだから，次の何れかがよい。

Positive: Orders are increasing rapidly; *therefore*(,) our stock is decreasing.

　　or　Orders are increasing rapidly. *Therefore*(,) our stock is decreasing.

　　or　Orders are increasing rapidly; our stock is decreasing.

(2)「当社の利潤は多少減りましたが，たいした問題ではありません」

Negative: Our profits have fallen slightly, *however*, this is not a serious problem.

Positive: Our profits have fallen slightly; *however*(,) this is not a serious problem.

 or Our profits have fallen slightly. *However*(,) this is not a serious problem.

 or Our profits have fallen slightly; this is not a serious problem.

(3)「新しいシステムは申し分なく作動しますので，古いシステムの倍はコストアップしなければならないでしょう」

Negative: The new system works satisfactorily, *therefore* we will have to increase the cost twice as much as the old system.

Positive: The new system works satisfactorily; *therefore* we will have to increase the cost twice as much as the old system.

 or The new system works satisfactorily. *Therefore* we will have to increase the cost twice as much as the old system.

 or The new system works satisfactorily, *and* we will *therefore* have to increase the cost twice as much as the old system.

1.8　注意すべき助動詞

　第二次大戦で D. MacArthur が日本軍に追われてフィリピンを去るときに，I shall return. (私は必ず戻ってくる) といった言葉は有名である。この shall の代わりに，他の助動詞を使ったのでは，敗北を認めたことになるので助動詞の選択は疎かにできない。

　「使ってみてください。きっと好きになるに違いありません」を，日本語に引っぱられて，Try it! You must like it! では「好きにならねばなりません」になるので，言われた方は Why! と問い返すであろう。You may (might) like it! では自信喪失を意味する。You will like it. がよい。このように助動詞一つで局面が変わるのでビジネスの世界では使う助動詞に注意しなければならない。

　「ご注文をいただいた品は10日以内に出荷いたします」を
　Your order shall be shipped within ten days.
では shall を使っているので契約書調になり，どんなことがあっても10日以内に出荷しなければならない決意を示すことになる。契約書でなければ shall は will にする。

① 「お友達に電話したければ，私の職場の電話を使ってください」

　Negative: If you *would like* to call your friend, please use the telephone in my office.

　would like to では，やや消極的で，電話をする気持ちが少ないような印象を与えかねない。

　Positive: If you *want* to call your friend, please use ～.

② 「システムを改善しようと思っておりますので，お気付きの点がございましたらご連絡ください」

　Negative: We want to improve our system, so please let us have any suggestions you *will* have.

　will を使っている。苦情に対する返事で，悪い点を知っていて，それを相手に指摘して貰おうとするなら好い。will だとユーザー (you) が99％このシステムの問題点を知っていることになり，ユ

ーザーは買ってくれないだろう。

Positive: We want to improve our system, so please let us have any suggestions you *may* have.

may よりも丁重に言うなら might。

③「ほかの容器をご使用になると，機械が壊れることがあります。その場合は当社の保証は無効になります」

Negative: Our guarantee is void if other containers are used, as this *may* damage your machine.

may では，50%以下の可能性で機械が壊れないことになるから，内容的には認めることができるが，他社の容器を使わせたくないならば，その助動詞は何が適切だろうかを考えよう。

Positive: Our guarantee is void if other containers are used, as this *will* damage your machine.

④「当社のシステムにご関心をお持ちいただき有り難うございました。他にお役に立つ事がご座いましたなら，是非ご連絡ください」

Negative: Let me thank you for your interest in our system, and if we *may* be of any further help to you, please contact us.

may だと，極めて消極的である。

Positive: Let me thank you for your interest in our system, and if we *can* be of any further help to you, 〜.

⑤「電気を入れて，メーターの目盛りを調べてください。正常ならば 0 を指す筈です」

Negative: Switch it on, and check the meter reading: if it's functioning correctly, the pointer *would* read 0.

would では2〜3％の可能性になってしまうので不可。

Positive: Switch it on, and check the meter reading: if it's functioning correctly, the pointer *should* read 0.
[さらに確証があれば should を must にする]

⑥「本状は，発送部における原料の積み方に二つの方法があり，その可能性を調査することを目的としています。」

Negative: The purpose of this letter *shall be to* examine the feasibility of two different methods of loading raw materials in the Shipping Department.

このような場合の shall は契約書に使うので，このような契約書でない文では不可。shall は慎重に使おう。

Positive: The purpose of this letter *is to* examine the feasibility of two different methods of loading raw materials in the shipping department.

⑦「お送り戴いた注文番号123の部品は返品いたします」

Negative: We *would like to* return the parts of the Order 123 you sent us.

would like to return では「受け取っても好い」ような印象を与える。本当に返品したい場合を考えよう。

Positive: We *are returning* the parts of the Order 123 you sent us.

⑧「当社は強力な販売網を持っておりますので，貴社製品は相当量さばくことができると思います」

Negative: As we have strong networks, we feel sure we *can* handle considerable quantities of your products.

can では自信があり過ぎる。may では自信がなさ過ぎる。

Positive: As we have strong networks, we feel sure we *will* be able to handle considerable quantities of your products. [will は shall でもよい]

⑨「もしその製品の情報を入手なさっておりませんでしたら，すぐお手紙を出した方がよいでしょう」

Negative: If you do not have the information on the product, you *had better* write to them at once.

had better では，あなたは手紙を出す義務がある (you *must* write) ととられ，義務感，脅迫感を与えることになる。

Positive: If you do not have the information on the product, please write to them right away.

⑩ 「これらの値段に魅力があることにお気付きになられ，恐らく直ぐにご注文がいただけるものと思います」

Negative: You have found these prices attractive, and *maybe* we *will* receive your orders very soon.

maybe ... will ～ では，Perhaps we will receive your order. にもなり，Perhaps we will not receive your order. にもなってしまう。maybe を安直に使わないように注意しよう。

Positive: You have found these prices attractive, and we *are looking forward to receiving* your orders very soon.

または

We are pleased to learn that you have found these prices attractive, and we *are looking forward to receiving* your orders very soon."

1.9　差別語を避ける

日本でもセクハラ (sexual harassment) 問題や差別語の使用が問われるご時世になった。年齢に関する差別語，人種に関する差別語，宗教上の差別語，身障者へ偏見を持つような差別語は使ってはならない。Avoid race, age, ethnic, religious, and disability biases in language. といわれている。アメリカ向けの手紙では，特に神経を使わなければならない。

男女の差別を避けて，代名詞で he か she かが分からないときには，he/she としたり，s/he と書く人もいる。

The Oxford English Dictionary (OED) は，he か she かが区別できないときは単数であっても複数の代名詞 they, their, them の使用を勧めて

いる。ここでは，使用を避けたい語と使用を勧める語とを対比する。詳しくは次の本が参考になる。

Casey Miller & Kate Swift: *The Handbook of Nonsexist Writing*, Harper Perennial, 2nd Edition, 1988

Margaret Doyle: *The A-Z of Non-Sexist Language*, The Women's Press Ltd., 1995.

使用を避けたい語（句）	使用を勧める語（句）
businessman	businessperson; executive; manager (*pl.* businesspeople)
cameraman	camera operator; photographer
fellowman	fellow citizens; fellow humans
If a man can	If someone can
foreman; forelady	supervisor
lady	woman
lady lawyer	lawyer
layout man	layout planner
longshoreman	docker; dockworker
mailman	mail carrier
male nurse	nurse
manager and wife	manager and spouse
manhandle	mistreat
manhours	operator-hours; worker-hours
mankind	humankind
manmade	artificial; manufactured; plastic; synthetic
manpower	human power; muscle power; personnel
Negress	black woman（年齢により異なる）
No man 〜.	No one 〜.
old people	senior citizens
policeman	police officer

serviceman	service engineer
statesmanlike	diplomatic
stewardess	flight attendant
waiter; waitress	wait person (*pl.* wait people)
weatherman	weathercaster
women's lib	feminist; women's movement
workingman	worker; wage earner
workmanlike	skillful

1.10　Subjectの書き方

　ビジネスレターが受信者に望ましい結果を与えるか否かは Subject (首題) の書き方で決まる。忙しい受信者は，手紙を読まないで内容を即座に知りたいものだ。Subject が書いてなかったり，曖昧に書かれていると，受信者は馬鹿にされている思いをする。どのように書かれた Subject が効果的であろうか。明確な Subject の要件として，J.C. Mathes & D.W. Stevenson: *Designing Technical Reports*: Allyn and Bacon, (1991)では次のよう書いている。

* 単語は一語一義で，主題と目的 (または書類の種類) を明確に述べているか。
* 読み手が理解出来る単語を使っているか。
* 10語以内が望ましい。
* 重要語は前へ出す。
* study of, report on, investigation of のようなあまりにも一般化し，曖昧な語句は使わない方がよい。

　以上は Short Report, Long Report, Research Paper を対象にしたものだが，ビジネスレターにも適用できよう。

　Negative:　Subject: <u>Portable Telephones</u>
　これでは主題だけで目的が書かれていないので，Portable Telephones

の何か，Portable Telephones をどうするのかが読み手に理解できない。そこで次のように目的を加えると明確になる。

> **Positive:** Subject: Purchase Order for Portable Telephones Model 99
> **Negative:** Subject: ABC Dumper

これでは主題も曖昧。目的も書いてない。何の Dumper だろうか。Dumper をどうしたのだろうか。主題を明確に表記し，目的を書くと分かりやすい。

> **Positive:** Subject: Improper Repairs on the ABC Rotary Car Dumper
> **Negative:** Subject: My Charge Account

これでは何の Charge Account か，また何時の Charge Account かが分からない。つまり主題が曖昧。また，My Charge Account の何か，My Charge Account をどうするのかの目的も書かれていない。これらの点を明確にすると次のようになる。

> **Positive:** Subject: Incorrect Statement on My November Charge Account No. 99-3454

1.11 パラグラフのまとめ方

　ビジネス分野の文章は受信者に読んでもらい，内容を理解してもらえなければ書いたことが徒労に終わる。そこで大切な要素にパラグラフがある。いかなる文書にもパラグラフがあり，パラグラフには，一つのまとまりと流れがある。まとまりがなく，流れのないパラグラフは，内容が汲み取れないばかりか，受信者に誤解を与えることが多い。

　一つのパラグラフに一つの主題 (One topic in one paragraph) いう原則を守ると内容は理解し易い。ビジネスレターでは文の流れにも注意をしなければならないが，大切な用件はできるかぎり最初のパラグラフに収めるようにも心がけよう。

第2章

ビジネスレターの構成

　手紙を発信した人の気持ちが受信者に真っ先に伝わるのが，使っているレターペーパー(用紙)と様式であろう。用紙と様式は受信者に与える第一印象といえる。第一印象が悪いと，手紙の内容が申し分なくても，受信者は読まないかもしれない。たとえ読んだとしても，こんな相手と仕事をすると，後々問題が起こり面倒だから返事は適当にしておこうという気持ちにさせ，ビジネスにつながるチャンスを失うことにもなりかねない。

2.1　レターペーパー (Letter Paper)

　レターペーパーは，罫線のない，良質のものがよい。質が悪いと会社の品位を落とす。社長や役員用は普通のレターペーパーと変え，特に良質のものにしている会社もある。社外用と社内用は当然区別するべきだろう。あまりにも厚かったり，逆に薄すぎたりする用紙は避けたほうがよい。

　レターペーパーの色は，白の無地か，クリーム，薄いグレイ，薄いピンク，薄緑などが無難である。強烈な印象を与える派手な色は避けるべきである。手紙の受信者に好印象を与える色がよい。

　2ページに互るとき，2ページ目からは Letterhead のない Blank Paper (白紙) を使うので，Letterhead つき Letter Paper と Blank Paper の2種類を準備しておくべきである。

　2ページ目からは次のように，社名・ページ・日付だけを Letter Paper の上部にタイプする。

| ACME Insurance Company | 2 | July 1, 20xx |

2.2 構成要素

2.2.1 必携項目

ビジネスレターでは構成要素 (Individual Parts of Business Letters) が決まっているので守らなければならない。

① **Letterhead**（レターヘッド）

(次例の左端の①〜⑦までは必携項目を，(a)〜(d) は任意項目を意味する)

会社のもう一つの顔ともいうべきところがレターヘッドである。ここには，社名 (Company Name)，住所 (Address)，電話番号 (Telephone Number)，ファックス番号 (FAX Number)，Eメール番号 (E-mail Address)，商標(Logotype)などを，通常は，用紙の上辺に書く。レターヘッド付きの用紙は公文書を意味するので私用には使わない。

      Wm. **WRIGLEY** Company
     Wholesome—Delicious—Satisfying

FAX:313-3213-2222
Phone:313-3213-0011
① 335 S. Ashland Ave.
Chicago, IL 60609-1234   (a) Your Ref: Our Ref:

② July 1, 20xx

③ Mr. John Doe
  Executive Director
  Investigation Lab Company
  123 Chemical Drive
  Analytical, IL 6666-1234
  U. S. A.

(b) Attn:

④ Dear Mr. Doe:

(c) Subject: <u>Format for Business Letters</u>

We here at Wrigley's are interested in developing more effective and efficient methods for analyzing chewing gum base. Our objective is to obtain accurate measurements of physical properties on the base.

⑤ We are requesting that you present a research proposal for the development of improved analytical methods.

We are looking forward to working with you. Please let us know if you would be willing to spend a day here, on a consulting basis, to discuss this request.

⑥ Sincerely,

(サイン)

⑦ William J. Wokas
Manager, Product Development Dept.

(d) JK:sf
(e) Enc.:map
(f) CC: Mr. Yoshio Arai
(g) PS: Please airmail your reply to me in a day or two.

② **Date (日付)**

通常，作成日をレターヘッドから2～4行下に書く。

* 手紙をタイプした日付けではなく，作成した日にする。
* 2行に書かないで1行に書く
* アメリカでは，通常，日に1*st*, 2*nd*, 3*rd*, 4*th* のような序数を表す接尾辞は付けない。
* Jan. とか Feb. のように月に略語を用いない。
* 3/7 とか 1/7 のように数字で書かない。この表示は March 7 か July 3 かが分からなかったり，国により月日の書き方が異なるからである。
* 格式ばった手紙のみ July fifteenth のようにスペルアウトする。

アメリカ式とイギリス式がある。

 アメリカ式 July 1, 20xx
 イギリス式 1st July 20xx

なお，アメリカ政府や軍隊では 1 July 20xx が使われている。

③ **Inside Address (書状内宛名)**

受信人の社名と住所を書くところである。通常，Date より2行ほど下の位置にタイプする。

 [例] Mr. Damon Kong
   The Bank of California
   400 California Street
   San Francisco, CA 94145-1234
   U. S. A.

* 相手が書いてきた通りにタイプする。

ACME Insurance Co. と書いてきたのを ACME Insurance Company としたり，B.G.Light, Inc. と書いてきたのを B.G.Light, Incorporated と書き直してはならない。社名の前に定冠詞が付いていれば必ず付けること。

* 受信者の男女の区別がつかないときは，Damon Kong のように敬称は付けなくてよい。

* 複数に宛てるときは，受信者の苗字をアルファベット順にタイプする。そして，一通の手紙を回し読みしてくれないので，タイプをした名前の全員にそれぞれコピーを送信する。

　[例]　Mr. J. C. Mathes
　　　　Mr. Dwight W. Stevenson
　　　　ACME Insurance Company
　　　　111 Main Street
　　　　Ann Arbor, MI 48109-2140

* 番地の前に，No. 50 Fifth Avenue のように No. のような不要語を付けてはならない。50 Fifth Avenue がよい。また，通常は，Room 305, 50 Fifth Avenue とせず，50 Fifth Avenue, Room 305 のように部屋番号は番地の次に書く。数字が重なるのを避けるためである。

* Room は Rm, East は E. と略してもよいが，スペースが十分あるときは，通常は略さない。

* 12 以下の数字の街路名 (Street & Avenue) はスペルアウトする。One 以外の家屋番号 (house number) は数字を用いる。

　　　Five South Twelfth Street　　　Room 101
　　　Five South 15 Street　　　　　Five Seventh Avenue
　　　One Park Avenue　　　　　　　123-67 Street

* 通常，市・区・町の後にコンマを打つ。アメリカは州名を次のような 2 文字の省略で表すのが普通である。州名には略語を使うが市 (City) は略さない。

United States Postal Service 発行の *Designing Business Letter Mail* では州名を次のような略語で示している。

American Samoa	AS	Kentucky	KY	Ohio	OH
Arkansas	AR	Louisiana	LA	Oklahoma	OK
Alabama	AL	Maine	ME	Oregon	OR
Alaska	AK	Marshall Islands	MH	Palau	PW
Arizona	AZ	Maryland	MD	Pennsylvania	PA
California	CA	Massachusetts	MA	Puerto Rico	PR
Colorado	CO	Michigan	MI	Rhode Island	RI
Connecticut	CT	Minnesota	MN	South Carolina	SC
Delaware	DE	Mississippi	MS	South Dakota	SD
District of Columbia		Missouri	MO	Tennessee	TN
	DC	Montana	MT	Texas	TX
Federated States of		Nebraska	NE	Utah	UT
Micronesia	FM	Nevada	NV	Vermont	VT
Florida	FL	New Hampshire	NH	Virginia	VA
Guam	GU	New Jersey	NJ	Virgin Islands	VI
Hawaii	HI	New Mexico	NM	Washington	WA
Idaho	ID	New York	NY	West Virginia	WV
Illinois	IL	North Carolina	NC	Wisconsin	WI
Indiana	IN	North Dakota	ND	Wyoming	WY
Iowa	IA	Northern Mariana			
Kansas	KS	Islands	MP		

* アメリカは，州名の後に 9 桁数字の ZIP (zone improvement plan の略) code (郵便番号) を付ける。最初の 5 桁は州と都市の配達局を示す。これにハイフンを付けて配達区域を示す 4 桁数字を続ける。

イギリスでは，アルファベットと数字を組み合わせた Postal Code (郵便番号) を用い，OX2 5UD のように表記する。最終行に，アメリカ宛なら U.S.A. (または USA) と，イギリス宛なら U.K. (または UK) とタイプする。

* Mr., Ms., Mrs. などは略称を用いるのが普通だが，President, Director, Manager, Secretary, Professor など敬称は省略しない。なお，Mr., Ms., Mrs. のあとのピリオドを省略する人もいる。

* 肩書きはできる限り名前と同じ行に続ける。長いときは名前の下に書く。

 Mr. Richard W. Roe, Chief Engineer
 ACME Engineering Company

* 人名の下の行に社名を書く。

* 社名の下に部署名を書く。

 Ms. Marina Charles
 ACME Engineering Company
 Technical Assistant

* 二つ以上の肩書きのある人に出すときは最高位の肩書きだけを書く。

United States Postal Service 発行の *Designing Business Letter Mail* では次のような略語を認めている。

(a) Direction (方向)

North	N	East	E	South	S
West	W	Northeast	NE	Southeast	SE
Southwest	SW	Northwest	NW		

(b) Secondary Address Unit (番地付帯項目)

Apartment	APT	Building	BLDG

(c) Street Designators (街表示)

Alley	ALY	Divide	DV	Ridge	RDG
Annex	ANX	Drive	DR	River	RIV
Arcade	ARC	Estates	EST	Road	RD
Avenue	AVE	Expressway	EXPY	Row	ROW
Bayou	BYU	Extension	EXT	Run	RUN
Beach	BCH	Fall	FALL	Shoal	SHL
Bend	BND	Falls	FLS	Shoals	SHLS
Bluff	BLF	Ferry	FRY	Shore	SHR
Bottom	BTM	Field	FLD	Shores	SHRS
Boulevard	BLVD	Fields	FLDS	Spring	SPGS
Branch	BR	Flats	FLT	Spur	SPUR
Bridge	BRG	Ford	FRD	Square	SQ
Brook	BRK	Forest	FRST	Station	STA
Burg	BG	Forge	FRG	Stravenue	STRA
Bypass	BYP	Fork	FRK	Stream	STRM
Camp	CP	Fort	FT	Street	ST
Canyon	CYN	Freeway	FWY	Summit	SMT
Cape	CPE	Gardens	GDNS	Terrace	TER
Causeway	CSWY	Gateway	GTWY	Trace	TRCE
Center	CTR	Glen	GLN	Track	TRAK
Circle	CIR	Green	GRN	Trail	TRL
Cliffs	CLFS	Grove	GRV	Trailer	TRLS
Club	CLB	Harbor	HBR	Tunnel	TUNL
Corner	COR	Haven	HVN	Turnpike	TPKE
Corners	CORS	Heights	HTS	Union	UN
Course	CRSE	Plains	PLNS	Valley	VLY
Court	CT	Plaza	PLZ	Viaduct	VIA
Courts	CTS	Point	PT	View	VW
Cove	CV	Port	PRT	Village	VLG
Creek	CRK	Prairie	PR	Ville	VL
Crescent	CRES	Radial	RADL	Vista	VIS
Crossing	XING	Ranch	RNCH	Walk	WALK
Dale	DL	Rapids	RPDS	Way	WAY
Dam	DM	Rest	RST	Wells	WLS

次に州名を書く位置を示す。

　　[例]　Mr. Damon Kong, Vice President
　　　　　The First Bank of California
　　　　　400 California Street
　　　　　San Francisco, CA　12345-6789
　　　　　U. S. A.

④ **Salutation** (挨拶文句)

「拝啓」に相当する。Inside Address より2行下にタイプする。

＊できる限り受信者の Family Name (姓) を書く。Mr., Mrs., Dr. 以外は略語は用いない。

　　　　Dear Mr. Smith:
　　　　Dear Mrs. Smith:
　　　　Dear Dr. Smith:
　　　　Dear Professor Smith: (Professor を Prof. のように省略しない)
　　　　Dear Ms. Smith: (受信者が既婚か未婚かが分からないとき)
　　　　Dear Miss Smith:

親しい間柄で，相手が First Name (名) で書いてきたら，こちらもそれに答えて First Name を用いるべきである。この場合は，敬称は付けず，またコロンではなくコンマになる。

　　　　Dear Dick,
　　　　Dear Tom,

＊相手の個人名は分からないが社名，部署名と肩書きが分かるときは，次のように書く。Salutation を併用した例を示す。

　　[例]　Manager of Personnel
　　　　　Acme Insurance Corporation
　　　　　Carew Towers
　　　　　300 E. Main ST　RM 1234
　　　　　Memphis, TN　38166-1121
　　　　　U. S. A.

　　　　　Dear Sir or Madam:

* 社名は分かるが個人名，部署名が分からないときは，次のように書く。Salutation と併用した例を示す。
    [例]　Newton Knitting Mills, Inc.
    　　　111 Belair DR　STE　402
    　　　Beverly Hills, CA　90210-3456
    　　　U. S. A.

    　　　Ladies and Gentlemen:

* 会社宛で受信者の名前が分からないときは，次の二通りのSalutationを用いた。

    Gentlemen: アメリカ式(コロンに注意)
    Dear Sirs, イギリス式(コンマに注意)

　しかし，差別主義者(sexist)と見られるのを避けるために，アメリカでは，Gentlemen: の代わりに Ladies and Gentlemen: を，個人宛なら Dear Sir / Ms: とか Dear Madam or Sir: を使う。また Dear Sales Manager:, To the Sales Manager:, Dear Commissioners:, To the Commissioners: のような肩書きでもよい。Dear All Nippon Airlines:, To All Nippon Airlines: のような社名でもよい。あるいは Dear Client:, Dear Reader:, Dear Sportsperson:, Dear New Car Owner:, Dear Member of ABC:, Dear Friends of J.A.P.E.; などを用いるようになった。最近ではイギリス人からの手紙でも Dear Sir / Madam, が見られる。

* 名前の後に敬称は付けない。

    Dear Mr. Mathes, Manager
    [Manager は不要]

* 名前から男女の区別が付かないときは敬称を付けないか，次例のように full name にするか，M. を付けるか，Mr. or Ms. とする。

    Dear Lee Smith:
    M. Jan Smith:
    Dear Mr. or Ms. Smith:

* 推薦状 (Letter of Recommendation) などのように受信人を特定できない場合は To Whom It May Concern: が普通だったが，今では Dear Director: とか Dear President: とか Dear Manager: などと宛先の部署の責任者の肩書きを英語で書くことが多くなった。

* 受領者が二人以上のときは複数形の敬称を用いる。

 [例1] Mr. J. C. Mathes
   Mr. Dwight W. Stevenson
   (Inside Address)

   Dear Messrs. Mathes and Stevenson:

 [例2] Ms. Margaret McLaren
   Ms. Leslie Olson
   (Inside Address)

   Dear Mses. McLaren and Olson:

 [例3] Mrs. Margaret McLaren
   Mrs. Leslie Olson
   (Inside Address)

   Dear Mmes. McLaren and Olson:

[Mmes. は Madam, Madame, Mrs. の複数形で Mesdames [meidάːm / méidæm] の略。

Return Address (差出人住所；返送先) 住所の書き方

日本から外国へ出す手紙の住所は，社名，部署，街区符号，住居番号，町名丁目，市町村名，都道府県，郵便番号，国名の順に，ローマ字で書く。

[例]　〒100-0111　東京都千代田区有楽町3丁目1番5号
　　　国際ビル234号
　　　平安貿易株式会社
　　　輸出部　奥島泰三

Taizo Okushima
Heian Trading Co., Ltd.
Export Department
Room 234, Kokusai Building
1-5　Yurakucho 3-chome
Chiyoda-ku, Tokyo
100-0111　Japan

個人なら次のように，通常，3行でまとめて書く。

[例]　〒187-0111東京都小平市仲町3丁目8番5号
　　　島田　芳雄

Yoshio Shimada
3-8-5　Naka-machi
Kodaira-shi, Tokyo
187-0111　Japan

マンション住まいは次のように書く。

[例]　〒187-0111　東京都小平市仲町2丁目4番6号
　　　葵荘　123号
　　　島田　美子

>Yoshiko Shimada
>Room 123, Aoi-so
>2-4-6 Naka-machi
>Kodaira-shi, Tokyo
>187-0111 Japan

＊町名，市，県などは英訳しない。
千葉県千葉市は Chiba City, Chiba Prefecture としないで，Chiba-shi か Chiba でよい。

＊番地を 4-3-2 と書くと，2丁目か4丁目かが分からなくなる懸念がでたら，

>3-2 Naka-machi 4-chome
>Kodaira-shi, Tokyo

と書く。2丁目3番地4号なら，3-4 Naka-machi 2-chome と書く。1丁目は 1-chome, 2丁目は Ni-chome, 3丁目は San-chome などと書いてもよい。

⑤ **Body of Letter** (本文)

話題が異なったら新しいパラグラフで始める。一つのまとまりでパラグラフを切る。つまり，One Topic in One Paragraph (1パラグラフに1主題)という原則に徹しよう。重要項目はできるだけ最初のパラグラフで述べるのが英文ビジネスレターの鉄則である。それぞれの Sample Letter を参照。

「貴社，益々ご清栄の段，心からお喜び申し上げます」とか「日頃は格別のご愛顧を賜り厚く御礼申し上げます」のような日本の手紙の常套文は英語の手紙にはないので英文にしないこと。

＊短い手紙はダブルスペースでタイプすると見栄えがする。
＊パラグラフとパラグラフの間はダブルスペース開ける。
＊アメリカ英語とイギリス英語を混ぜない。アメリカ宛ならアメリカ英語を，イギリス宛ならイギリス英語に統一する。
＊月の前に日を書くときは，seventh of July とか 7th of July のように日をスペルアウトするか日に序数を付ける。

* 月と年の間はコンマは不要である。
July 2000 とし July, 2000 としない。
* ハイフンのつなぎ場所を間違えないように。単語を切るときは辞書でハイフンの位置を確認すること。

⑥ **Complimentary Close (Closing)** (結び文句)

　「敬具」に相当する。ビジネスレターでは必ず書くが，ファクシミリや E-mail で Salutation を書かないときは，Complimentary Close も不要である。

* 最初の単語は大文字で始める。
* 最後の単語の後にコンマを付ける。
* truly を truely と書くようなミススペルや，respectfully を respectively と書くような誤りを避ける。
* アメリカでは次が普通である。

　　Sincerely,　　　　Sincerely yours,　　　Very sincerely yours,
　　Cordially,　　　　Cordially yours,　　　Very cordially yours,

次は格式張った場合に用いる。
　　Yours very truly,　Very truly yours,
　　Respectfully yours, は畏敬の念を抱く人に用いる。

次は形式ばらないで略式の場合に用いる。
　　Best wishes,　　　Kindest regards,　　　Warmest regards,
　　As ever,　　　　　Cheers!　　　　　　　See you in Tokyo!

イギリスでは次が普通である。
　　Yours faithfully,　　Faithfully yours,　　Very truly yours,
　　Yours very truly,　　Yours truly,

George E. Parker: *Handbook of Model Letters & Memos* (Prentice Hall) では Salutations と Complimentary Closes の関係を次ぎのように整理している。

	Salutations	**Complimentary Closes**
Very Formal:	My dear Sir:	Respectfully,
	Sir:	Yours respectfully,
	My dear Madam:	Respectfully,
	Madam:	Yours respectfully,
Formal:	Dear Sir:	Very truly yours,
	Dear Madam:	Yours very truly,
	Gentlemen:	Yours truly,
	Ladies:	Very truly yours,
Less Formal:	Dear Mr. Suchard:	Sincerely,
	Dear Ms. Sheehan:	Sincerely yours,
	Dear Dr. Lubow:	Yours sincerely,
Personal:	Dear Mr. Suchard:	Yours cordially,
	Dear Ms. Sheehan:	Cordially,
	Dear Dr. Lubow:	Cordially yours,

ビジネスでは，Less Formal が Formal より好まれる，と述べている参考書が多い。また，Personal は個人的色彩が濃いと述べている。

⑦ **Signature** (署名)

一度決めたサインは変えてはならないので，しっかりと練習し，恥ずかしくない書体で書くように練習しておこう。

* Letterhead に社名が印刷してあるビジネスレターでは，Signature のすぐ上に社名をタイプする必要はない。Letterhead に，サインをする人の名前が書いてあれば，署名欄には名前をタイプしない。
* 肩書きは，氏名の1行下にタイプする。
* 部署名はタイプされた氏名か肩書きの1行下にタイプする。
* 通常はタイプされている名前の人がサインする。
* Complimentary Close から2行ほど下に氏名をタイプし，氏名の1〜2行ほど上部にサインをする。

[例]　Sincerely,
　　　(サイン)
　　　Yoshio Maruyama

男女の区別を明確にしたければ次の方法がよい。

[例]　Sincerely,　　　　　　Sincerely,
　　　(サイン)　　　　　　　(サイン)
　　　Mr. Marumi Maruyama　Miss Marumi Maruyama

女性で未婚を打ち出したければ，次の方法がよい。

[例]　Sincerely,
　　　(サイン)
　　　Miss Akiko Marui

既婚・未婚を隠したければ，次の書き方をする。

[例]　Sincerely,
　　　(サイン)
　　　Ms. Akiko Marui

既婚とか未亡人とかを言いたければ，次の書き方をする。

[例]　Sincerely,
　　　(サイン)
　　　Mrs. Kimiko Marui

代理署名は，できる限り避けたほうがよいが止むを得ない場合は，署名の前に By か Per を付けるか，社名をタイプして，その前に For か p.p. を書くのが普通である。p.p. は per procuration の略。

[例]

By　(サイン)　　　　　　　For WASEDA CORPORATION
　Eiichi Marui　　　　　　　(サイン)
　　　　　　　　　　　　　Shintaro Ishihara
　　　　　　　　　　　　　Manager, Sales Department

2.2.2 任意項目

次の各項目はビジネスレターの任意項目 (Optional Elements) となっているが，使うと便利である。

(a) Reference Number (参照欄)

商社は数多くの商品を扱い，数多くの得意先に対して，何度も問合わせるので，出す手紙 (outgoing letter) には Reference Number を付けておくと相手からの来状 (incoming letter) と照合するのに時間の節約になる。文書保管の上からも便利といえよう。受取った手紙に Reference Number が明記してあれば，返信状にもその Reference Number をタイプしなければならない。

通常，先方の Reference Number を Your Ref. と書いて相手の番号をタイプし，自分の Reference Number は Our Ref. と書いて自分の番号をタイプする。

Letterhead に In reply please refer to ..... と書いてあれば，この後に発信者の Reference Number を Our Reference #1234 のようにタイプする。

通常はレターヘッドの右下欄に書く。

    Your Ref. 20-0202
    Our Ref. 12-0118

(b) Attention Line (特定名宛人欄)

Particular Address ともいう。会社宛の通信文で，特定商品を宛先の担当者が分からないときとか，担当部署が分からないときに，来状の署名者宛にすると迅速に処理をしてくれるばかりか，親近感も沸くであろう。会社宛だと読み手が不明確なので放置される懸念がでる。このような場合とか，団体を「気付け」として通信文を託送したい場合に書く。この受信人が不在のときは，来社するまで開封されない恐れもあるのが欠点である。

Inside Address の下に1行余分に空けて，Attention: か，Attention of か [省略して Attn.]，次に受信者の名前をタイプする。封筒にも明記する。なお，この場合の Salutation は，アメリカなら Ladies and

Gentlemen: とし，イギリスなら Dear Sirs, とする。

　[例]　　ACME Insurance, Inc.
　　　　　Carew Towers
　　　　　300 E. Main St. Rm 1234
　　　　　Memphis, TN 38166-1121
　　　　　U. S. A.

　　　　　Attention: Mr. Dwight W. Stevenson

　　　　　Ladies and Gentlemen:

(c) Subject Line（件名欄）
　「件名」に相当する。件名に内容が明記してあると忙しい役職者とかビジネスマンは，通信文の本文を読まなくても概要が把握できたり，後日の参照にも便利なので，できる限り書くことを勧める。書き方については「1.10 Subject (首題) の書き方」(30ページ) 参照。
＊通常は，Salutation の下に2行あけてタイプする。手紙では Salutation の前にタイプしない。
＊内容語だけを大文字で始める。
＊下線を施す。2行にまたがるときは最後の行だけに下線を施す。
　次の方法のどれかを使う。

　[例1]
　　　　　Dear Mr. Charles:
　　　　　　　　<u>Shipment of Your Order 123</u>

　　　　　Thank you for your detailed and thoughtful letter in response to our....

[例2] Subject にコロンを付け，その後に続ける。多用されている。
 Dear Mr. Smith:
  Subject: <u>Shipment of Your Order 123</u>

 Sometimes we find a product or service so worthwhile that ....

[例3]　Re にコロンを付け，それに続ける。
 Dear Mr. Smith:
  Re: <u>Shipment of Your Order 123</u>

 We are pleased to inform you that effective January 27, 20xx, our ....

なお，re はラテン語の in re の re だけを用いたものだから省略のピリオッドは付けないがコロンは付けるのが普通である。英語では regarding に当たる。短いので，ファクシミリや E-mail で好んで使われる。

(d) Identification Marks（文責者とタイピスト名記入欄）
　タイピストを使って手紙を作成する場合，署名者とタイピストの頭文字 (initial) を書き，責任を明らかにする欄である。日本には3人で1通の手紙の責任を持つメーカーがあるが，この場合は，最高責任者 (通常はサインをする人)，文責者，タイピスト，それぞれ3者の頭文字をタイプする。署名者の名前の頭文字は大文字が普通だが，タイピストの頭文字は小文字にすることもある。省略のピリオッドは付けない。
　なお，自分で手紙を作成し，タイプするときは，この欄は不要である。Identification Marks の位置は，Signature より2行ほど下にタイプする。

 [例]　　MS/ys　　MS:ys　　MS/YS/tk　　MS:ys:tk

(e) Enclosure（同封物記入欄）
　通信文に同封物があるとき，出状者がそれを明記する欄で，受信者も確認ができるので便利である。Identification Marks の下に次のようにタイプする。

>Enc: Catalog

複数あるときは

>Encs: Catalog and Price List

とタイプする。Enc. は Encl. でもよい。

(f) Carbon Copy Notation (写しの送付先)

　手紙の写しを関係先へ送付したことを送信者へ伝える欄で，送付先はいくつ書いてもよい。Original ではなく複写した手紙を送るのでサインはしなくてよい。サインをする場所に / s / か / S / とタイプして，このあとにサインをする人の名前をタイプするタイピストもいる。

　CC (cc と小文字でもよい) は carbon copy の略。現在では carbon でコピーを取らないので courtesy copies と言う人もいる。コピーを作るにはコピー機を使って photocopy (写真複写) するのが普通なので，c とか copy とか pc の略語を使っている企業もある。しかし，従来から CC が多用されている。省略のピリオドは付けないでコロンを付ける。

　[例]　　cc:　Mr. Dwight W. Stevenson

　　　　　CC:　Mr. J. C. Mathes
　　　　　　　 Mr. Dwight W. Stevenson

　　　　　Copy to Mr. Dwight W. Stevenson

　　　　　Copies to Mr. J. C. Mathes
　　　　　　　　　 Mr. Dwight W. Stevenson

　二人以上に送るときは CC: か Copies to を用いて，肩書きの高い方から低い方への順にするか，苗字をアルファベット順に並べるのが普通である。

　First name か initials で始まる名前では，次のように，Mr., Ms., Mrs., Miss などの敬称は省略してよい。

cc: Dwight W. Stevenson　　　CC: J. C. Mathes
  　　　　　　　　　　　　　　　W. I. Smith

 他人へコピーを転送したことが手紙の受信人に分かっては困るときに Blind Carbon Copy (略: bcc——発信した証拠の残らない手紙の写し)を使う。bcc とか bcc: の次に CC と同じ方式で名前をタイプするが,手紙の original, つまり,宛名人に行く手紙にはタイプしないで,コピーの方だけにタイプする。Xc とタイプする人もいるが Xerox copy (ゼロクスコピー)と間違えられるので用いない方がよいとされている。

(g) Postscript (追伸)

 従来は,本文を書き終えた段階で,書き忘れた事柄や新たに入手した情報などを付記するのに利用した。しかしワープロを使う今日では,どこにも自由に挿入ができるので従来からの用法ではなく,事柄を強調したいときにこの欄を利用するようになった。

 Signature から2行下に P.S. と書いて強調したいことを書く。p.s. でも,PS でも P.S. でもよい。なお,「追追伸」は post postscript といい,PPS と略して用いる。

2.3　様式 (Format for Business Letters)

　ビジネスレターで使われている様式は Full Block Style, Block Style, Semiblock Style, Indented Style であるが，近ごろは Simplified Style に人気がある。

　Full Block Style は，全ての項目を左のマージンに揃えてタイプするので，能率がよく，アメリカ人が好む。しかし横着な印象を与え，見た目がよくないと非難する人もいる。

[例]

② ＿＿＿＿＿＿
③ ＿＿＿＿＿＿
　　＿＿＿＿＿＿
　　＿＿＿＿＿＿

④ ＿＿＿＿＿＿
⑤ ＿＿＿＿＿＿＿＿＿＿＿＿＿＿＿＿＿＿＿＿＿＿＿＿＿＿＿
　　＿＿＿＿＿＿＿＿＿＿＿＿＿＿＿＿＿＿＿＿＿＿＿＿＿＿＿
　　＿＿＿＿＿＿＿＿＿＿＿＿＿＿＿＿＿＿＿＿＿＿＿＿＿＿＿
　　＿＿＿＿＿＿＿＿＿＿＿＿＿＿＿＿＿＿＿＿＿＿＿＿＿＿＿
　　＿＿＿＿＿＿＿＿＿＿＿＿＿＿＿＿＿＿＿＿＿＿＿＿＿＿＿

⑥ ＿＿＿＿＿＿
⑦ ＿＿＿＿＿＿
　　＿＿＿＿＿＿

　Block Style は，Inside Address, Salutation, Body は左のマージンに揃えてタイプし，Date, Complimentary Close, Signature の位置をレターペーパーのほぼ真ん中から揃えてタイプする様式である。

[例]

　　　　　　　　　　　　　　　　② ＿＿＿＿＿＿

③ ＿＿＿＿＿＿
　＿＿＿＿＿＿
　＿＿＿＿＿＿
④ ＿＿＿＿＿＿
⑤ ＿＿＿＿＿＿
　　＿＿＿＿＿＿＿＿＿＿＿＿＿＿＿＿＿
　　＿＿＿＿＿＿＿＿＿＿＿＿＿＿＿＿＿
　　＿＿＿＿＿＿＿＿＿＿＿＿＿＿＿＿＿
　　＿＿＿＿＿＿＿＿＿＿＿＿＿＿＿＿＿
　　＿＿＿＿＿＿＿＿＿＿＿＿＿＿＿＿＿
　　　　　　　　　　　　⑥ ＿＿＿＿＿＿

　　　　　　　　　　　　⑦ ＿＿＿＿＿＿
　　　　　　　　　　　　　＿＿＿＿＿＿

　Semiblock Style は，Block Style とほぼ同じだが，本文のそれぞれのパラグラフの始めを3文字から5文字ほど引っ込めてタイプをする様式である（例省略）。

　Indented Style は，Semiblock Style とほぼ同じだが，Inside Address の2行目を2文字から3文字ほど引っ込め，3行目，4行目を2行目と同じくらい引っ込めながらタイプしていく様式。Signature Line も Complimentary Close より2～3文字引っ込めてタイプする。この方式は手が掛かるので招待状や案内状などの格式張った手紙に用いられる。

[例]

② ＿＿＿＿＿＿

③ ＿＿＿＿＿＿
　　……＿＿＿＿＿＿
　　　……＿＿＿＿＿＿＿＿
④ ＿＿＿＿＿＿
⑤ ……＿＿＿＿＿＿＿＿＿＿＿＿＿＿＿＿＿＿＿＿＿＿＿＿
　　＿＿＿＿＿＿＿＿＿＿＿＿＿＿＿＿＿＿＿＿＿＿＿＿
　　＿＿＿＿＿＿＿＿＿＿＿＿＿＿＿＿＿＿＿＿＿＿＿＿
　　……＿＿＿＿＿＿＿＿＿＿＿＿＿＿＿＿＿＿＿＿＿＿

⑥ ＿＿＿＿＿＿
⑦ ＿＿＿＿＿＿
　　……＿＿＿＿＿＿＿
　　　……＿＿＿＿＿＿＿

　Simplified Style は「簡略型」で，Full Block Style とほぼ同じだが，Salutation も Complimentary Close も省略するところが異なる。男性・女性の区分の必要もないので煩わしくないが，ドライな印象を与える。ファクシミリや E-mail のような Informal な場合に多用されている。

　いずれの様式を使っても自由だが，混用してはならない。混用すると，人格が疑われるし，受信人を惑わすので，一つの様式に一貫した方がよい。

2.4 句読法 (Punctuation Patterns in Business Letters)

Letterhead や様式が手紙の受信者へ発信者のイメージ，つまり企業のイメージを強烈に与えるように，句読法もいい加減だと企業のイメージダウンにつながるので注意が肝要である。

Open-Punctuation Pattern (句読点省略型), Mixed-Punctuation Pattern (句読点混合型), Closed-Punctuation Pattern (句読点厳守型) があるが，いずれを使用するかは企業サイドで決める問題である。様式により用いる句読法にも決まりがある。

Open-Punctuation Pattern では，Date, Inside Address, Body は普通の句読法だが，Salutation の後，Complimentary Close の後の句読点を省略する形で，Full Block Style で用いる。

Mixed-Punctuation Pattern では，それぞれの項ですでに説明をしたような句読法にする。Block Style や Semiblock Style で用い，最も一般的である。

Closed Punctuation は，主として，イギリス (ヨーロッパ) で用いられ，本文 (Body) の句読法は，Open-Punctuation や Mixed Punctuation と同じだが，Date, Inside Address, Signature Line の最後にそれぞれ Period を付ける。主として Indented Style で用いる。

[例]   18th July 20xx.

　　　Mr. Robert Gibbons,
　　　　Sherfield Hall,
　　　　　200 Northcourt Ave.,
　　　　　　Reading RG20 7EY,
　　　　　　　England.

　　　Dear Mr. Gibbons,

I am very pleased to ＿＿＿＿＿（本文）＿＿＿＿＿

           Yours faithfully,

          （サイン省略）
          Susumu Kato
           Export Department.

2.5 封筒 (Envelope)

　レターペーパーと同じ紙質・色の封筒を使う。封筒は，レターペーパーと同様，差出人の第一印象を与えるので大切な部分である。
　封筒には，Return Address (差出人住所)，Mail Address (宛先)，Mail Direction (手紙指示事項) を所定の位置にタイプする。自分勝手に位置を変えて，Mail Address を封筒の真ん中にタイプし，その下に Return Address をタイプすると，手紙が宛先に配達されないで下に書いてある住所，つまり発信者に配達されるので注意。発信者に戻ってくることになる。Return Address と Mail Address の書き方はすでに述べたので，ここでは Mail Direction について説明する。

2.5.1　Mail Direction
　次のような英語を用いる。
　Air Mail (航空便)，Sea Mail (船便) [アメリカでは Surface とか Surface Mail という]，Special Delivery (速達) [Express ともいう]，Registered (書留)，Printed Matter (印刷物)，Catalog Only (カタログ在中)，Photo Only (写真在中)。　住所の位置，次頁参照。

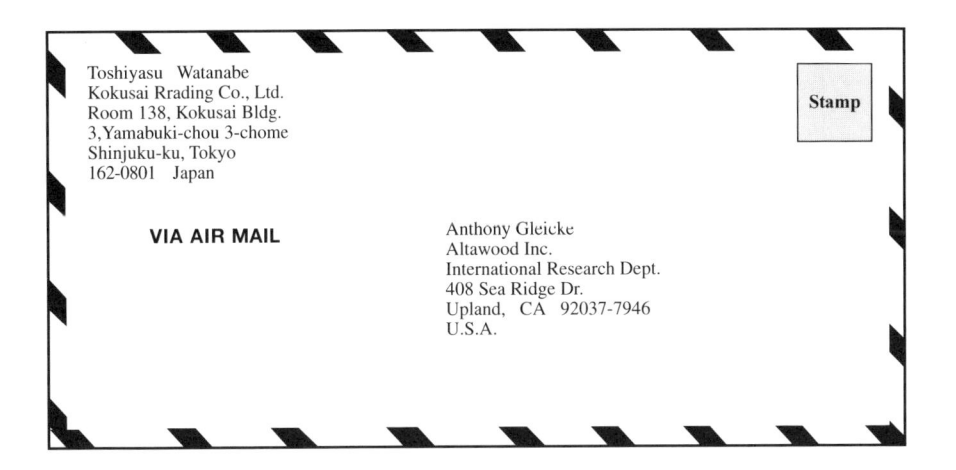

```
Toshiyasu  Watanabe
Kokusai Rrading Co., Ltd.
Room 138, Kokusai Bldg.
3,Yamabuki-chou 3-chome
Shinjuku-ku, Tokyo
162-0801  Japan                                              Stamp


        VIA AIR MAIL        Anthony Gleicke
                            Altawood Inc.
                            International Research Dept.
                            408 Sea Ridge Dr.
                            Upland, CA  92037-7946
                            U.S.A.
```

2.5.2　折り方

　レターペーパーは，通常，2つ折りか3つ折りにして封筒へ入れる。二つ折りの場合は真ん中で折ればよいが，三つ折りでは，次のように折って封筒へ入れる。

（1）レターペーパーの下方より1/3ほどの所で内側に上方へ折る。

（2）上方より1/3ほどの所で下方へ折る。

（3）封筒を開けて，裏側を上に向けて左手で持つ。

（4）折った手紙は最後に折った折り目を下にして，右手で封筒へ入れる。

　レターペーパーが三つ折りにしても封筒へ入らないときは，最初に1/2ほどで上方に折り，次に左右より，それぞれ1/3ぐらいの所で内側に三つ折りにする。　（次頁の図参照）

① ② ③ ④

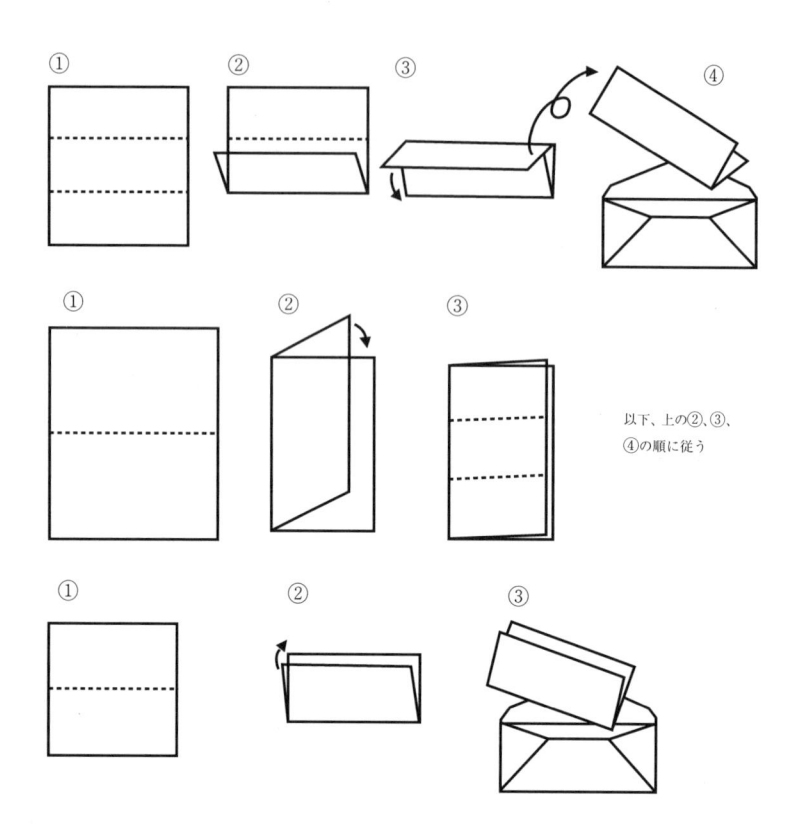

① ② ③ 以下、上の②、③、④の順に従う

① ② ③

第3章

取引申込み

3.1 引合い (1)

　買手が売手に売申込みなどを依頼するときの買手の問合せや要求を引合い (Inquiry) という。商品のカタログを請求した簡単なものから、買手が関心を持つ商品の価格表や見本などを請求するもの、価格に関する問合せや納期を問合わせるものなどがある。また、商品の仕入の可否を尋ねたり、包装、保険、支払方法、商品の性能などを問い合わせたものもある。通常は、買手と売手との最初の接点となる手紙である。

3.1.1 内容構成

　次のような内容構成が普通であるが、初めての手紙ならば、明確、簡潔、丁重に書くように心掛ける。

　　＊ 初めて売手に出す手紙には売手の名前の入手先を明記する。
　　＊ 買手が売手に求める希望事項を明記する。
　　＊ 支払方法を知らせる。
　　＊ 自社を紹介する。

書く順序に決まりがあるわけではない。用件の重要度にしたがって、重要なものから書き進んでいくのが原則といえよう。どう書けば効果があるかを考えながら書くことに終始するとよい。必要でない事柄は書かないように。受信者が逆に発信者に問い合わせたりすることがないように注意しなければならない。

　通常、次の7項目を明記する。

　　（１）　品名 (Commodity Name)。必要に応じて明細 (Description) も明記する。
　　（２）　数量 (Quantity)
　　（３）　価格 (Price)
　　（４）　納期 (Delivery Date; Time of Shipment)

（5） 支払条件 (Terms of Payment)
（6） 保険 (Insurance)
（7） 荷造り；梱包方法 (Mode of Packing)

3.1.2　例文

[Sample letter 1]

Ladies and Gentlemen:

We have seen, according to your advertisement in the May 5th issue of *Time*, that you handle sophisticated digital cameras.

Please send us a complete catalogue of your cameras by airmail, together with your export terms and conditions.

We are established importers and distributors of a wide variety of cameras and office equipment, including personal computers and printers.

Our bank is The Bank of Heisei, which, we are sure, will provide you with information about our financial standing.

We look forward to your early response.

Sincerely,

　　　【注】We have seen 〜 は We have read 〜 でも We have learned でもよい。according to は，ここでは from でもよい。May 5th issue（5月号）。*Time* 雑誌名や書物名はイタリックにする。イタリック体がないときは下線を引く。sophisticated「精巧な」。highly *sophisticated machine*（極めて精巧な機械）。第二パラグラフで直ぐ用件を述べていることに注意。Please send 〜 は I would like to ask you to send 〜

では要求が弱すぎる。complete = total (一式の)。together with (と共に) は多用される。terms and conditions「取引条件」。terms だけでもよい。established「老舗の」= long-established; old-established。importers and distributors「輸入兼販売業者」。「相手の注意を引くために Importers and Distributors のように大文字で始めることがある。distributor については次例参照。We だから importers and distributors と複数形にしている。a wide variety of (多種類の) は好んで使われる。office equipment「事務器」equipment は単数形で用いる。Our bank「当社の取引銀行」。which は who でもよい。financial standing「財政状態」。look forward to には名詞か動名詞が続き動詞は続かない。

[Sample letter 2]

Ladies and Gentlemen:

We have learned from The Chamber of Commerce and Industry in your city that you are looking for a distributor of your automobile accessories in Japan. We would like to fill that position.

Since ours is a trading company with offices both in Japan and abroad, as well as close connections with many Japanese retail stores throughout Japan, we can assure you that your products will be made widely available in this country.

For our business and credit standing, we may refer you to The Bank of Heisei, Marunouchi, Tokyo.

Your prompt reply would be appreciated.

Sincerely,

【注】 The Chamber of Commerce and Industry「商工会議所」(米では The Chamber of Commerce「商業会議所」という)。are looking for 〜「〜を探している」。distributor「特約店」。詳しくは 95 ページ参照。automobile accessories「自動車の付属品」 fill = fulfil「務める」。since は because や as よりも格式張った英語。ours = our company。a trading company「(貿易) 商社」offices in Japan and abroad「国の内外に会社 (を持つ)」。office については次例の注を参照。close connections with〜「〜と綿密な関係」。retail store「小売店」。be widely available「大いに需要がある」。For our business and credit standing「当社の営業状態と信用状態については」。we may refer you to 〜 は please refer to より丁重。Your prompt reply would be appreciated. は We would appreciate your prompt reply. よりも丁重。

[Sample letter 3]

Ladies and Gentlemen:

I found your firm listed in one of the United States Trade Lists indicating that you are interested in handling magnetic recording media.

Hi-Tech Company, Inc. is among the largest manufacturers of magnetic recording media such as floppy disks, optical disks, computer tapes, memory cards, cassettes, etc. in Japan. We manufacture a full line of magnetic recording media. Please find literature enclosed describing our products.

If you are interested, please reply by return, giving us some information on your product lines and your methods of distribution.

Sincerely,

Tohru Saito

Export Sales Manager

TS / sn
Encl. Current catalog

PS　I will be in your country from March 12 to March 16 and will stay at the Pacific Hotel. Please be kind enough to contact me.
PPS　I'll be leaving New York for Canada on March 17.

【注】firm「会社」。一般に, 大小を問わず商社, 商会を firm といい, company は物を製造または販売する会社をさす。corporation は米国で好まれ, 一般に法人化された会社をさす。株式会社は Corporation のほかに米国では Inc. (Incorporated の略), 英国では Ltd. (Limitedの略) を用いる。英国では PLC; plc (Public Limited Company の略) を用いることもある。なお,「会社で仕事をする」などのように仕事をする場所を意味するときは office を用いる。「私はまだ会社にいます」は I am still at the office. が普通。 listed は直前に which was を挿入して考える。indicating ～ は which indicates ～ と考える。handling = selling。magnetic recording media「磁気記録媒体」。「当社は」に We や Our Company ではなく Hi-Tech Company, Inc. と社名を用いたのは相手に社名を印象づけたかったから。among the largest manufacturers とは one of the largest manufacturers のこと。manufacturer は「メーカー」。maker は個人を指すことが多いので, 企業を指すときは manufacturer が好ましい。optical disks「光デスク」。memory cards「記憶カード; メモリーカード」。cassettes = cassette tapes。manufacture は produce; make のこと。a full line of ～「～の全商品に亙る」line = range (米)。Please find literature enclosed とは We enclose (or are enclosing) literature より勿体ぶった表現。literature とは catalog とか brochure のこと。しかし, literature の方が格好がいい。your methods of distribution = your sales and marketing methods。PS (= postscript 追伸) は P.S.; p.s. とも略すが PS が多用されている。PPS (=post, postscript 追追伸) については 55 ページ参照。

3.2　引合い（2）

　「引合い (1)」では，初めて取引を申し出た手紙の例を中心とした。この課では，すでに取引関係が成立している相手企業に問い合わせる例を紹介する。

　すでにお互いに手紙を交換したことがあるので文面もビジネスライクになるのが普通である。要件のみを明記することに終始し，不必要な事柄は書かないように注意しよう。

　実際のビジネスでは，何回も手紙を交換している人や，すでに面識のある人に出状するケースが圧倒的に多いといえよう。

　すでに取引関係にある企業に出す引合状の作成にあたっては，次の点に注意をしよう。

3.2.1　内容構成

* 首題 (Subject) を付ける。

　首題を読むだけで受信者は内容が即座に理解できるので，忙しいビジネスマンは時間の節約ができる。「1.10 Subject の書き方」(p. 30) を参照。

* Salutation は個人名にする。

　Gentlemen: とか Dear Sirs, のような不特定な人に宛てた Salutation では，責任逃れをされたり，返事が早く貰えなかったりすることが多い。

* ビジネスライクな英語にする。

　すでに手紙を交換しているのだから，丁寧すぎたり，あまりにもへりくだった英語を使うと相手は訝しく思い，警戒してくることがあるので注意しよう。

* 冒頭から具体的な内容を書く。

　We have an inquiry from the ABC Company for your Portable Telephones. (貴社の携帯電話の引合いが ABC Company からありました) のような書出しでもよい。

* 尋ねる項目が多いときは箇条書きがよい。

大切な要件から箇条書きにすると読み手はいらいらしなくてすむ。

3.2.2 例文

[Sample letter 4]

Dear Mr. Rash:

Re: <u>Request for information about Stylus-10</u>

We are pleased to inform you that the Kowa Co., Ltd. is considering buying a new electronic computer for the calculations necessary in the design of optical lenses.

To this end we have been requested by the company to secure information about the following points to help them in the selection of the appropriate model for their company. The company is interested only in information restricted to U.S. sales.

1. Ratio of Stylus-10 to all computers being adopted by companies in the optical business in the U.S.A., and the number of Stylus-10's adopted.
2. Names of companies in the optical business who are adopting Stylus-10 and the dates of delivery.
3. Principal kinds of calculating and programming being done by these companies.
4. One or two instances illustrating the calculating efficiency between the Stylus-10 and other computers.
5. Approximate maintenance expenses of Stylus-10 per year, and average rate of depreciation.
6. Possibility and ease of updating software.

7. Any data showing the superiority of the Stylus-10 in optical calculations compared with others.

We look forward to hearing from you soon.

Sincerely,

> 【注】We are pleased to については「1.2 Softener が大切」を参照。necessary は直前の calculations を修飾する。in the design of optical lenses 「光学レンズの設計に」。To this end「この目的のために」。find information about ~「~について情報を見つける」。appropriate「適切な」。restricted to U.S. sales「米国で販売されたものに限る」。restricted は直前の information を修飾する。Ratio of ~ to ...「~と...の割合」。adopted「採用された」。the dates of delivery「納期」。Principal = main; chief。illustrating = showing。calculating efficiency「計算の効率」。Approximate = estimated; rough。maintenance expenses [保守費]。average「平均の」。depreciation「減価償却」。updating「最新の」。superiority「優位 (な点)」。optical calculations 「光学計算」。「look forward to + 名詞か動名詞」に注意。

[Sample letter 5]

Ladies and Gentlemen:

Subject: Request for Clave Calculating Adjustment Manuals and Parts Catalogs

Please send me, if at all possible, a copy each of your adjustment manuals and Parts Catalogs for all models of Clave Calculating Machines.

If this cannot be done, I would like to request information as to where these manuals and catalogs can be obtained.

As it stands now, I have not been able to locate anyone here with any manuals nor information as to where they can be obtained. Therefore, I have many machines not in operating condition.

Kind consideration to this letter will be deeply appreciated.

Sincerely yours,

【注】 本状も極めて businesslike な例である。要件を無駄なく，てきぱき述べている。この返事は [Sample letter 9] に示す。a copy of と the copy of の違いは [Sample letter 6] の注を参照。adjustment manuals「調整マニュアル」。Parts Catalogs「部品カタログ」。サービスマンが主として利用する部品名や部品番号が書かれているカタログ。if at all possible「ともかく出来れば」if it is possible の短縮形に at all (= in any way) を挿入した形。as to where は格式張った用法で where だけでよい。As it stands now = Up to this point (現時点まで)。not ～ nor ...の両方の打消し構文に注意。locate = find (見出す)。Kind consideration to this letter will be deeply appreciated. は丁重な結び。困っていることを露骨に出したいために丁重過ぎる結びで終えたものだろう。I would appreciate your kind consideration to this letter. が普通。

第4章 取引申込みの返事

　買手からの引合いに対して売手は迅速に返信する (reply to inquiry) のが定石である。この返信が長期的な大きいビジネスにつながることにもなるからである。また，ビジネスマンたる者が定石を無視したり，ルールを守らない返事を出したりしたのでは，相手から嘲笑されて，真面目に対応してもらえず，商取引のチャンスも失いかねない。

　返事をするのに調査をしたり，検討したりする時間がかかると思ったときは無回答のままにしておかないで，取りあえずお礼の返事を出すべきである。引合い先への新しい出状なので丁重な語調がよい。引合いの返信では売申込み (Offer) をすることが多い。

4.1　内容構成

　引合いの返信を書く要領は次の通りである。
* 引合い状をいただいたお礼を述べる。
* 相手からの照会事項をどのように処理をしたかを述べる。相手が問い合わせてきた順に回答する。
* 相手が照会してきた商品には，当社の製品が最高 (the finest quality) のような説明を加え，購買意欲を促す。

　　We are very proud of the system, and we believe you will find it to be the most effective and efficient. （当社はそのシステムを非常に誇りとしておりますので，貴殿もきっと効果があがり，能率のあがるシステムであることに気が付くでしょう）のような文を書く。
* 注文なり，返事を待っているような結びの文で終える。あるいは次のような文で終えてもよい

　　If we can be of any further help to you, please contact us.
　（当社がお役に立てることがございましたなら，ご連絡ください）

4.2　例文

[Sample letter 6]

Dear Mr. Sinclair:

We were very pleased to learn from your May 5 letter that you have read our advertisement in a recent issue of the *Time*.

As requested, we are sending you a copy of our latest illustrated catalog together with a price list.

We are very enthusiastic about the new model, as we have incorporated some entirely new features.

Because we are the manufacturers of many other office machines, ranging from desktop personal computers to general computers, we have also enclosed for your consideration a copy of our current general catalog.

Please let us know if we may be of further assistance.

Sincerely,

【注】We were very pleased to ... は We were very glad ... よりは格調が高く，It is our great pleasure to ...よりは格調が低い。「1.2 Softener が大切」を参照。We were very pleased to learn from 〜. の代わりに We have learned from 〜 that ...の構文も多用される。As requested「ご要求の通り」。we are sending 〜と進行形を用いて誠意を示している。we will send 〜では誠意を欠く。a copy of (〜1枚) と the copy of (〜の写し) を混同しないように。illustrated catalog「図解入りカタログ」。英では catalogue と綴る。together with は with だけ

でもよい。price list「値段表」。We are very enthusiastic about 〜「当社は 〜 (の開発) に熱中している」。we have incorporated in 〜「〜 に組入れる」。features「特徴」。we are manufacturers of many other office machines 〜 はwe manufacture many other office machines 〜 のこと。office machine「事務用機械」。ranging from 〜 to ...「〜 から...にわたる範囲で」。desktop「卓上型の」。general computer「汎用コンピューター」。for your consideration (ご参考までに) は挿入句。general catalog「総合カタログ」。

　この手紙が個人宛ならば，Please let us know 〜 assistance. の前に次のような文を続けることができる。

　Should you decide to place an order, you may use the convenient order form in the center of the catalog. (ご注文をくださることをお決めになりましたなら，カタログの真ん中にある便利な注文用紙をお使いください)

be of further assistance = help you further。

[Sample letter 7]

Dear Mr. Stevenson:

Thank you for your letter of May 5 requesting us to send you our latest catalog for men's wear.

As requested, we have enclosed our general catalog in which all men's wear as well as women's wear are illustrated. You will notice that we do our utmost to maintain our reputation for quality and reliability. Therefore we are sure that all our products will meet your requirements.

We have also enclosed the terms and conditions for exporting our goods. Please note our special 5% introductory discount on orders of fifty or more items.

Owing to expanded business, we now carry a larger stock. Therefore, we will be able to dispatch the goods to you within two weeks after receipt of the order.

We very much look forward to doing business with you.

Sincerely,

【注】 〜 your letter of May 5 requesting us to 〜 は 〜 your letter in which you requested us to 〜 でもよい。We have enclosed 〜（〜を同封する）は多用されるので覚えておくとよい。We enclose でもよい。general catalog「総合カタログ」。You will notice that ... は will が使われているので確実性を打ち出している。You will see that ... では see だから弱い。do our utmost to [do]「当社は [〜をしようと] 最善を尽くす」。to maintain our reputation for 〜「〜に対する評判を維持する」。quality「品質の良いこと」。reliability「信頼性」。meet your requirements「貴社のご要求に答える」。terms and conditions は terms（条件）だけでもよい。Please note 〜 は You will notice 〜 だと弱くなる。introductory discount「キャンペーン中の割引[価格]」。fifty or more items は「50品目以上」のこと。more than fifty items だと「51品目から」になる。dispatch = send。look forward to には動詞か動名詞が続く。

[Sample letter 8]

Dear Mr. Heath:

Subject: <u>Ref. # S-893 - Reply to inquiry</u>

We apologize for the delay in answering your letter of March 11. We would like to inform you that we are the exclusive distributors of Mz Water Treatment Equipment in Japan. Therefore, we would be happy to supply the products at U.S. Government prices if you have the proper tax-exemption documentation. I am enclosing our current price list.

In reply to your questions:

1. Delivery is made to you at U.S. Government prices (with proper tax-exemption documents); free delivery.
2. Delivery is made within 120 days of your firm order.
3. Maintenance facilities and parts are available in Japan.
4. Six-month guarantee including free parts and service (based on normal use).
5. Used machines, even Sines, are not accepted as trade-ins. (A list of suitable firms will be supplied upon request.)

Thank you for your patronage, and we hope we can be of service to you in the future.

Sincerely,

第4章　取引申込みの返事

【注】本状は Inquiry の返事と Offer (売申込み) を兼ねた例である。実際にはこの種の内容の手紙が多い。We apologize for the delay ～「～することに遅れて申し訳ございませんでした」。決まり文句。We must apologize for not replying sooner to your letter. とも書く。exclusive distributors「一手販売店」。we だから distributors と複数形にした。海外の輸出業者が当該商品を輸入業者以外には輸出しないという契約を結んだ業者を exclusive distributor という。次章参照。Mz Water Treatment Equipment「ミズ処理装置」。Mz は「水」からの造語。we would be happy to ～ は語調を柔らかくするために使ったもの。proper = correct; right; suitable。tax-exemption documentation「免税証明書類」。documentation = proof in the form of documents。free delivery「配達費無料」。firm order「確定注文；期限指定注文」。期限内に現品を指定の場所に引き渡すことを条件にした注文で、期限後は引き渡しを拒否できる。maintenance facilities「保守設備」。parts are available in ～「部品は ～ で入手できる」。free parts and service「部品とサービス無料」。on normal use「通常の使用で」。Sines は水処理機の製品名。trade-ins「下取り」。upon request「ご要求があれば」。patronage「ご愛顧」。

[Sample letter 9]

Dear Mr. Hullenbaugh:

Subject: Request for Autoclave Parts Catalog

Regarding your letter of July 20, we apologize for not being able to fulfill your request for the Adjustment Manual and Parts Catalog for Clave Calculating Machines, which unfortunately are unavailable at this time.
We would like to inform you of the address of Clave Calculating Company as follows.

The Clave Calculating Company
P.O. Box 1234

Bellmore, NY 11710
U. S. A.

Please feel free to contact them directly.

Again, we regret that we are unable to meet your request.

Sincerely,

【注】[Sample Letter 5] の返事である。Regarding は As for とか With でもよい。Concerning は長くて堅苦しいので使わない方がよいと警告している参考書もある。～ July 20 の次に requesting the Adjustment Manual and Parts Catalog ～ を続けてもよい。we apologize for not ... は謝るときの常套文。fulfill = carry out (果たす; 遂行する)。unavailable「手持ちがない」。inform you of the address ～ は give you the address でもよい。feel free to contact ～「遠慮なく連絡を取ってください」。feel free は命令文に用いられて「遠慮なく～する」。them は The Clave Calculating Company を指している。We regret ～ は相手の要求に答えられないときに用いられる常套文。通例 that を付ける。「1.4 打消しよりも肯定で」を参照。meet your request「ご要求に応ずる」

第5章

オファー

引合いを通じて売手, 買手のどちらかが, 実際の取引開始に向けて取引条件を相手に申込むことを Offer という。「申込み」と和訳するが, 英語の「オファー」のまま使用することが多い。一般には売手が買手に出すオファーが多く, これをを Selling Offer (売りオファー)といい, 買手が売手に出すオファーを Buying Offer (買いオファー) という。

オファーに承諾 (acceptance) があれば契約 (Contract) が成立する。オファーで大切なことは, 有効期限 (validity) である。無期限だと, 忘れたころに注文がきて, 値段やその他の条件が変わっていても, それに従はなければならない恐れがでる。

5.1 種類と英文の特徴

オファーには次のような種類がある。
(1) Free Offer (回答期限のないオファー)
(2) Firm Offer (ファームオファー; 確定オファー)
(3) Offer subject to confirmation (確認条件付きオファー)
(4) Offer subject to prior sale (またはOffer subject to being unsold) (先売り御免オファー; 売違い御免オファー)
(5) Offer on approval (点検売買オファー)
(6) Offer on sale or return (残品引取り条件付きオファー)

次にそれぞれを説明する。
(1) Free Offer (回答期限のないオファー)
　　このオファーも適正な (reasonable) 期間内に承諾がなければ失効する。
(2) Firm Offer (ファームオファー; 確定オファー)

貿易で最も多い方式。商品・納期・価格などの条件を定めて，回答期限を付けて申込むもので，期限が切れるまで申込者は申込みの修正・変更や撤回・取消しができない。

　　We offer firm, subject to your reply being received here by twelve noon on April 10 ....(貴社のご返事が4月10日正午までに当方に必着を条件として・・・を確定オファーします) のような英語を使う。Being sent ではなく being received (当方に必着する) と書いていることに注意。

　　We offer firm subject to your acceptance reaching us by 6:00 p.m. on April 10 .... (貴社のご承諾が4月10日午後6時までに必着を条件として・・・を確定オファーします) でもよい。

(3) Offer subject to confirmation (確認条件付きオファー)

　　価格の変動が激しい場合，相手が承認しても，申込者が最終的に確認しないと契約が成立しないオファーもある。subject to our (final) confirmation (当方の最終確認を条件として) も多用される。これらは，俗に sub-con offer (サブコンオファー) という。かつては offer without engagement (確約しないオファー) も用いられた。

(4) Offer subject to prior sale (または Offer subject to being unsold) (先売り御免オファー；売違い御免オファー)

　　販売数量が限られている在庫品を同じ条件で，客先に同時に発信するオファー。早い者勝ちで，他へ売ってしまうかもしれないことを断っているオファー。

(5) Offer on approval (点検売買オファー)

　　実物を実際に点検するか，使ってみて契約するか否かをきめるオファー。貿易では通常は用いない。

(6) Offer on sale or return (残品引取り条件付きオファー)

　　売れ残った品は引取るという条件付き。貿易では通常は用いない。

5.2 例文

[Sample letter 10]

Dear Mr. Branch:

Thank you very much for your April 15 inquiry, in reply to which we are pleased to make the following offer, subject to our final confirmation.

Item:	Stainless Steel Cylinders, TG type
	Bore sizes: 22 mm. Tandem style
Unit price:	$500
	FOB Japanese port in US currency
Quantity:	300
Shipment:	Within 3 months after receipt of your order and L/C
Packing:	1 unit to a box

For your information, our cylinders have enjoyed excellent sales in Japan, and therefore we are confident that they will be well received in your market as well.

We hope this offer is acceptable to you.

Sincerely,

【注】 〜 April 15 inquiry で切って，We are pleased to make 〜 としてもよいが，前文との関連を密接にしたいため Sample のように in reply to which で二文を続けた。in reply to which は in reply to the inquiry のこと。we are pleased to については「1.2 Softener が大切」を参照。subject to our final confirmation「当社の最終確認を条件として」。Item「品目；種目」。Description でもよい。Bore「内径」。Tandem style「タンデム　スタイル；縦に連結したスタイル」。Unit Price「単価」。$500と書き，$500.00のようにセントのゼロは付けない。FOB については 119 ページ参照。US currency「米通貨」。Quantity「数量」。L/C については 126 ページ参照）。Packing「包装」。1 unit to a box「一箱に一個詰め」。boxはcontainer でもよい。For your information「ご参考までに」。メモなどでは FYI と省略することが多い。therefore we are confident that 〜 の we are confident that は we are sure that 〜 の気持ちだが sure では自信を持ちすぎる。they will be の will に注意。may などでは自信がないことになる。be well received in your market「貴市場では人気がある」。We hope this offer is acceptable to you. はWe urge you to give some thought to this offer.のことだが，これでは「このご提供にご一考いただけますれば幸甚です」になり，少し弱い印象を与えるので例文のようにした。

[Sample letter 11]

Dear Mr. Wainwright:

In response to your inquiry of January 10, we immediately contacted Suzuki Metal Industries, Ltd. and succeeded in obtaining the following offer for one used blast furnace subject to prior sale.

    Description: Heian heavy-duty Furnace, Type EG-95
                     Details are specified in the attached leaflet
                     Reconditioned with a 1 year guarantee
    Price: Jp ￥10,000,000
    Terms: 1 / 2 by bank transfer on contract
                     1 / 2 by draft at sight on installation
                     Our service engineer will be stationed at the site during the first three months.
    Shipment: One month after initial payment

The furnace being offered this time was installed five years ago in Wakayama Works in Japan. Since the iron and steel industry here is in very bad shape, the manufacturer was forced to limit production. This is one of the reasons that Suzuki has decided to sell the furnace abroad.

Since this offer answers your urgent request, we recommend that you accept it.

Sincerely,

【注】In response to ～ (～へのご返事として) はよく使われる。response は answer よりも堅い語。With regard to や As for ～, Concerning ～ で始めてもよい。blast furnace「溶鉱炉」。subject to prior sale「先売り御免を条件として」。heavy-duty「頑丈な; 高性能な」, 通例, 名詞の前に置く。leaflet「ちらし」。Reconditioned「修理調整し新品と同様にした」。used machine (中古の機械) を再調整した機械類を reconditioned (machine) という。used よりも相手に好印象を与える。guarantee「保証」。Jp = Japanese。CIF は 119 ページ参照。Terms「支払条件」。ここでは 2 回払いになっている。1 回目は by bank transfer (銀行送金で) という条件。on contract (契約時に)。2 回目は by draft at sight (一覧払為替手形で)で on installation (据付け時) という条件。station「駐在する」。site「現場」。after initial payment「初回金受取り後」。in very bad shape「景気がとても悪い」。was forced to ～「～を余儀なくされた」。limit its production「生産を制限する」。this offer とは this counter offer のこと。we recommend that you accept it. を We *would like to* recommend that you accept it. のようにイタリックの部分を書くと一層丁寧になり, 場合によっては意志表示が弱い印象を与えることになる。

第6章

オファーへの返事

　オファーを手にした側は，自社に有利な条件をいろいろ付けて返信 (reply to offer) してくるのが普通である。通常，次の「種類と対処法」で述べる3通りが考えられる。

6.1 種類と対処法

(1) 条件通り承諾する
(2) 条件の変更を申し出る
(3) 見送る

　(1) の承諾 (acceptance) をするときは，期間内にオファーを受けた条件で受諾することを申込者に伝える。受諾により契約が成立する。通常，売手は「売約書 (Sale Note)」を，買手は「買約書 (Purchase Note)」を作成する。あるいは，「注文請書 (Acceptance of Order) [「注文承諾書 (Acknowledgment of Order)」とか「注文確認書 (Confirmation of Order)」ともいう]を買手に送付する。

　(2) は，オファーを受けた側がオファーされた値段・納期・数量などの一部か全部の条件の変更を申し出るケースである。これを Counter Offer「カウンター・オファー；逆オファー；反対オファー」という。実際には，何回もカウンター・オファーが双方から出て商談が成立することが多い。

　(3) は，条件がまったく合わないような場合で，拒絶の回答をすることによりオファーは消滅する。なお，返事をしなければ自然消滅する。

6.2 例文

[Sample letter 12]

Dear Mr. Johnson:

Thank you for your letter of May 15, offering your services for processing patent applications.

As a small company, we do not have the personnel to deal with such matters. For the last five years we have been depending on a company such as yours, and are quite pleased with it.

Should, however, we find a need for your services, we will keep your firm in mind and will contact you.

Sincerely,

【注】相手の申し出をソフトに断っている点に注意。offering は which offers のことだから直前にコンマを付けた方がよい。your services for processing 〜「〜を扱う貴社のサービス」。patent applications.「パテント申請」。personnel「職員」。deal with 〜「〜を扱う」。depending on は utilizing; employing the services of のこと。Should, however, we find a need for your services, は If, however, we should find a need for your services, のことだが, Although we have no immediate requirement for your services, では強すぎて失礼になることがある。keep your firm in mind「貴社を心に留めておく」。will contact you に when such a need arises in the future (将来そのような必要が生じたときには) のような文を続けると蛇足になる。

第6章　オファーへの返事

[Sample letter 13]

Dear Mr. Jones:

With your fax message No. 20-4545 in hand, we immediately took the matter up with our prospective buyer, but they are not interested in your price. They state that they have received from another source in Japan a much more attractive offer: about 10% below your price.

We know that your products are of high quality, but price is the most important issue now in our market. Will you therefore please contact your supplier again to see if they will reduce their price by 10%?

We look forward to receiving your favorable reply.

Sincerely,

【注】Counter Offer の例。With your fax message in hand「貴社のファックスを入手して」。付帯状況の with で通例「with ＋ 目的語 ＋ 副詞(句) [または, 形容詞か分詞]」の形で用いる。[例] Don't speak to your customers *with* your hands *in your pockets*. (両手をポケットに入れたままでお客に話しかけてはならない)。took (the matter) up with ～「(その件) を～と相談する」take ... up with ～ = ask ～ about ...。our prospective buyer「当社の見込み客」。state は say より堅い語。another source「別の筋」。of high quality = excellent。issue = subject to be talked about (問題点; 核心)。if は whether (...かどうか) よりも口語的用法。will は can でもよい。they = the supplier。by 10% = to the degree of 10%。程度を表す by。[例] I missed the train *by* five minutes yesterday. (昨日, 私は5分のところで列車に乗り遅れた)

第7章 代理店

ビジネスをするには，取引を希望する相手を発見し，取引の申込み (business proposition) をしなければならない。「取引申込状」は a letter proposing business というが，この手紙の中に，当方を代理店に指定して欲しいという単刀直入の申し込みもある。この課では代理店についての例文を検討する。

7.1 種類

貿易取引を目的とする代理店には，販売代理店 (selling agent) と買付代理店 (buying agent) がある。販売代理店には輸入する国に存在する海外販売代理店 (foreign selling agent) と輸出する国に存在する輸出代理店 (export sales agent) とがある。海外販売代理店は独占権が与えられている場合が多いため，総代理店 (sole agent) とか一手販売代理店 (exclusive selling agent) という。貿易取引で販売代理店というと foreign selling agent をさす。

輸出商と輸入商社で代理店についての話し合いがすむと両当事者間で代理店契約 (agency agreement) を結ぶのが普通である。

7.2 AgentとDistributor

通常，ある特定の一地域に一社に限定して営業活動を独占的に与えた商社を一手販売代理店 (sole agent) という。一定期間内に決められた売り上げをあげないと代理店契約を解除されることがある。Sole agent に似た一手販売店にディストリビューター (distributor) がある。ディストリビューターは本人 (principal) の立場である。輸入した製品を国内で卸売りをする輸入商で代理店ではない。工業製品や耐久消費財を取り扱い，プレ・サービスやアフター・サービスをするため修理工場，展示

場，サービス技術者などを抱えている。通常は「一手販売権契約」(exclusive distributorship agreement) を結び，協定した地域に一手販売権が与えられる。そして輸出先のメーカーと情報を交換したり，セールス活動をする。他社の製品，つまり競業品は扱えないように約定しているのが一般的である。

　契約書には，当事者の名称，所在地，契約の発効日のほかに，契約期間，品目，地域，権利，義務，手数料，契約解除の条件，紛争解決などの条項 (terms and conditions of contract) が記載される。

7.3　例文

[Sample letter 14]

Dear Mr. Mollis,

　We understand that you may be interested in the representation of our products in Japan.

　For your information we enclose the latest literature on our products and representative samples of the PERSONAL AIR PURIFICATION SYSTEM along with our leaflet on coated wires. In addition, we would like to point out that we supply NICOTINE ABSORBER CARTRIDGE, AUTOMOTIVE ACCESSORIES.

　Should you be interested in handling our range on a distributorship basis, we would welcome your comments with, if possible, an indication of the expected yearly turnover.

Yours faithfully,

【注】 We understand that 〜 (当社は〜だと了解いたしました) は返事の書き出しに多用され、丁寧な表現。you may であって you will でないことに注意。will だと確定的になって失礼になる。「1.8 注意すべき助動詞」を参照。representation は agent より格式の高い英語。For your information 「ご参考までに」。literature 「(カタログやパンフレットなどの) 印刷物」。representative samples 「代表的なサンプル」。PERSONAL AIR PURIFICATION SYSTEM とは「ポータブル型空気清浄器」のことを system と大袈裟に称している。強調のために商品名を大文字で表すことがある。along with は and と考えてよい。leaflet 「折込み印刷物；チラシ」。coated wires 「被覆線」。NICOTINE ABSORBER CARTRIDGE 「ニコチン吸い取りカートリッヂ」。AUTOMOTIVE ACCESSORIES. 「自動車の付属品」。range 「品目」 [米]では line。on a distributorship basis 「代理店として」。on a 〜 basis は多用される。we would welcome your comments 〜. は Please give us your comments 〜. より丁重な表現。ここから最後までは、We would be happy if you would let us know how many of the products you think that you can sell each year. のこと。turnover 「取引高 [量]」

[Sample letter 15]

Dear Mr. Gabbins:

Subject: <u>Reply to request for EH Air Compressor and Agent in US</u>

Thank you very much for your letter of April 20, in which you request information on our EH Air Compressor. You also query as to whether we have an agent in the U.S.

We are pleased to inform you that we are exclusively represented in your country by Odakison International Inc. Unfortunately, at this time we are not marketing the EH Model in the U.S., but we would recommend that you make contact with our dealer. We are writing him in the meantime and advising him of your interest.

Thank you again for writing us.

Yours sincerely,

Toshio Kato
Manager,
International Department

CC: Mr. James Seiler

> 【注】Subject の効果的な書き方を身につけること「1.10 Subject の書き方」を参照。〜 in which (本状の中で...) はよく用いられる構文。in which you request 〜 は requesting 〜 でもよい。query = question。request も query も現在形を使っていることに注意。過去だと過ぎてしまったことになる。as to whether は堅苦しい表現で whether だけでよい。if は whether より堅苦しくない。We are pleased to inform you that はほとんど意味がない。単刀直入に表現するのを避けている。We are glad to let you know that よりも堅い表現。We are exclusively represented by 〜「〜社が当社の一手代理店になっている」。「1.2 Softener が大切」を参照。make contact with は contact だけが簡潔。dealer = agent。him は dealer を指すので them でもよい。advising him は letting him know のほうが口語。この一文は We have written to the dealer informing him of your interest. が簡潔でよい。

[Sample letter 16]

Ladies and Gentlemen:

Subject: <u>Request for names and addresses of Monroe agents in Brazil</u>

Would you let us know by return airmail the name and address of your agent among the mountains in the Rio de Janeiro area? If this is inconvenient at this time, we would appreciate receiving the name and address of the Win agent in Rio de Janeiro as soon as possible.

We have been informed by the Yawata Iron & Steel Co., Ltd. that one Monroe computer purchased from us here in Japan will be sent to their Usiminas works in Brazil and that, out of the necessity of services and adjustments, they wish to know the name and address of your agent in that area whom they may contact when needed. Therefore, we would be happy to receive the complete list at your earliest convenience.

We look forward to hearing from you soon.

Sincerely,

【注】Monroe は computer の計算機名。worldwide「世界中にある」。Would you let us know ～? は Please let us know ～. より丁重な表現。初めての手紙なので丁重な表現を使っている。「1.1 大切な語調」を参照。by return airmail「折り返し航空便で」。among the mountains「山地にある」inconvenient「面倒な」。we would appreciate receiving the name ～. は please send us the name ～. より丁重な表現。the Yawata Iron & Steel Co., Ltd. の後に one of our customers を入れてもよい。 out of the necessity of services and adjustments「サ

ービスと調整の必要性から」。we would be happy to receive the complete list ～ は please send us the complete list ～ より丁重な表現。at your earliest convenience「ご都合つき次第」

[Sample letter 17]

Mr. Robert Brown   June 2, 20xx
Helmes Corporation
303 Fifth Avenue
New York 16, NY 10005

Dear Mr. Brown:

      Subject: Setting up a distributor in Japan

Your letter directed to Ishida Power System Corporation has been turned over to us for attention and reply, as we handle export matters for the company.

At the present time we do not have an agent or distributor in the U.S. and would be interested in working out an arrangement with your company whereby you could act as our distributor in your country.

We enclose descriptive and illustrative literature on both the already well-known line of "ZAP Power System" and the newest member of the family. The system assists the bicyclist when going uphill and during commutes, at speeds of up to 29.97 km/hr. It includes a powerful, lightweight motor system, maintenance-free battery, battery case, quick charger, and 3-speed controller. It is ideal for bicycle commuters. The product comes with a 1-year warranty.

Your offices in your country would, of course, require at least one or two systems as this is naturally the only truly effective way of selling it. If, after demonstrating the bicycles, your company would then wish to place an order for a minimum of 100, we could consider working with you as our distributor, and on that basis, we would be pleased to offer you the following discounts from the list prices shown in the enclosed circular:

    On "Powerbike" · · · · 30%
    On Other Systems · · · 20%

In all cases, shipment could be made within four to eight weeks after receipt of your order.

Normally our terms are cash with order or Letter of Credit, for which we allow a 2% discount. However, if payment is to be effected through our offices in your country, we could consider granting terms of 2% for payment within 10 days, or net 30 days.

We are writing this letter in duplicate, and all enclosures are also in duplicate, so that you may forward the duplicate letter and one set of enclosures to your offices in Southeast Asia.

We will be most interested in hearing from you once you have had an opportunity to study the information contained in this letter and the enclosed material. We hope you will find all the data and explanations you require, but should you need any further information, please let us know as we will be pleased to forward it immediately.

It would be very gratifying for us to be able to work with your company as our distributors in the areas you serve. We trust that your reply will enable us to complete the arrangements for doing so and to have the pleasure of shipping your initial order in the near future.

Very truly yours,

Taro Ishikawa
Manager

AD/lk
encl. descriptive and illustrative literature

【注】この手紙は全体に格式高い英語で書かれている。まず，相手の会社からの問合わせに明確に答えていることに注意しよう。このような考え方を真似るとよい。setting up = establishing; arranging。directed to ～「～へ宛てられた」。has been turned over to ～ = has been given to ～。for attention and reply「注意を促し，返事をするために」。export matters「輸出物質；輸出品」。do not have ～ or .... は not ～ or ... の構文に注意。working out an arrangement with your company「貴社と取決めを纏めあげる」とは「貴社を特約店にするように働きかける」こと。whereby は so that の格式高い表現。

　　　We enclose ～ を Enclosed you will find ～ とすると古い表現だと注意されることがあろう。descriptive and illustrative literature「説明・図解印刷物」。well-known line「よく知られた製品；有名な製品」。line = a type of goods [例] a new type of hats (新しいタイプの帽子)。family「グループ」。system とは「自転車」のこと。electric power systems「電動方式」。going uphill「上り道をこぐ」。during commutes「通勤途中」。km/hr は「毎時～キロ」のことで kilometers per hour と読む。includes a powerful, lightweight motor system「強力で軽量なモーターシステムを内蔵する」。maintenance-free「保守の必要がない」。quick charger「急速充電器」。3-speed controller「3段切替制御装置」。comes with ～「～付き」[例] The room comes with bath, air conditioning, and a refrigerator (部屋にはバス・トイレ，冷

暖房，冷蔵庫が付いている)。a 1-year warranty「１年の保証」[例] The manufacturers will have to repair the bicycle without charge because it is still under warranty. (自転車はまだ保証期間中なのでメーカーは無料で修理をしなければならないでしょう)

Your offices「貴社」。after demonstrating ～「～を現物で実際に説明した後で」。to place an order for a minimum of 100「最低100台の注文をする」。place an order for ～ は多用される。list prices「表記(してある) 値段」price list「値段表」とは異なる。

shipment could be made を we could ship ～ と書いていないことに注意。within four to eight weeks after receipt of your order (受注後4～8週間以内) は多用される構文。

with order「注文と共に」。Letter of Credit「信用状」L/Cと略す。たんに「クレジット」ともいう。be effected through ～ 格式張った言い方で「～ をとおして行われる」。granting も格式張った語で giving と同義。terms of 2% for payment within 10 days「10日以内のお支払いには２％の値引きという条件」。2% for payment は 2% discount for payment のこと。net 30 days は without discount within 30 days のこと。

in duplicate「２枚複写で」。forward は send の格式張った語。

should you need ? = if you should need ～。It would be very gratifying for us to ～ は We would be very pleased to よりも格式張った表現。trust は believe よりも格式張った語。initial order「初注文」。

第8章

注文とその返事

　買手が注文をし，売手が受諾 (acceptance of order) すれば契約となる。貿易では，手紙で確認したり，逆オファーの (1) で説明した注文書 (Order Sheet) で確認するのが普通である。

8.1　注文書の記載事項

　正式な注文書 (Purchase Order Sheet; P.O. Sheet) を受取った売手は売買契約書 (Sales Contract)，または売約書 (Sales Note) などの契約書を作成して，署名して買手に2部送付するのが普通である。

　通例，次の事項を記載する。

　商品の銘柄 (Description)，数量 (Quantity)，値段 (Price)，納期 (Delivery Date; Date of Shipment)，運送・保険の指図 (Freight・Insurance)，荷造り・荷印 (Packing・Marking)，支払方法 (Payment) など。

8.2　例文

[Sample letter 18]

Dear Ms. Karlin:

In reply to your letter of August 10, we are pleased to place an order by way of trial for "Waterwise 2000," Model ST. Enclosed is our Order No. 20-4502.　For your information, description and terms are as follows:

　　1.　Description: Waterwise 2000, Model ST.　Countertop

		Steam Distillation System. Removable Electric Cord. Removable Boiler. Stops automatically when the cycle is finished. With 4-liter Collector/Dispenser Bottle. Source: 100-120V, AC, 50-60 cycles.
2.	Q'ty:	5 units
3.	Price:	U.S. $500 each, CIF Yokohama
4.	Shipment:	During October to Kobe port

Please note that we are going to instruct our banker to open an Irrevocable L / C for the amount of this order.

We hope that you will expedite delivery of this order as the buyers are badly in need of the equipment.

Please confirm our order and reply as soon as possible by fax.

Sincerely,

【注】In reply to 〜「〜への(ご)返事として」。we are pleased to 〜 については「1.2 Softener が大切」を参照。place an order for 〜「〜の注文をする」。「本を本屋に注文する」は place an order for a book with a bookstore の構文を使う。しかし，place an order with a firm for a book でも，give an order for a book to a bookstore でも give an order to a bookstore for a book でもよい。I ordered a book for him. = I ordered him a book. とすると「私は彼に本を注文してやった」になる。「本屋に本を注文した」なら I ordered a book (to be sent) from a bookstore. [( ) 内は省略するのが普通]と書く。これを I ordered a book to a bookstore. と書くと，「私は本を本屋へ送ることを命令した」になる。by way of trial は「トライアルとして[のつもりで]；「試買注文で」。Waterwise とは Steam Distillation System (蒸気蒸留機器) のこと。For your information (ご参考までに) は多用される。description and terms「明細と条件」。Removable Electric Cord「取

外し可能なコード」。Removable Boiler「取外し可能な給湯器」。the cycle is finished「一工程が終了すると」。Collector / Dispenser Bottle「収集・取出しビン」。Source「電源」。Q'tyはQuantity (量) の略。unit「台数」, to openはto establish (開設する) も使える。our banker「当社の取引銀行」。an Irrevocable L / C「取消不能信用状」。126ページ参照。expedite = speed up。confirm our order「当注文をご確認する」。by fax「ファクシミリで」

[Sample letter 19]

Ladies and Gentlemen:

 Subject: <u>Book Order</u>

Please send me one (1) copy of:
 Author: Sandra Stevenson
 Title: *Verbs for a Specific Purpose*
    Published by Prentice-Hall, Inc., Englewood Cliffs, NJ 07632
 ISBN: 0-00-112345-X
 Payment: Please charge my Master Card # 1111-0009-9999-0011
    Valid thru: 09/20
 Ship to: Please send it by surface mail.

As I have been a satisfied customer for many years, I trust that you have my name and address in your records.

Sincerely,

Tomoko Motohashi

【注】簡単な注文書の例である。絶対に送って欲しいので Please send me ～ で始めている。これを I would like to ask you to send ～ とすると気乗りしない印象を与えることになる。書名はイタリックで書く。ISBN = International Standard Book Number (国際標準図書番号)。Payment「支払(法)」。charge my Master Card～「私のマスターカードに勘定を付ける」とは「マスターカードで支払する」こと。by surface mail[米]「船便で」, [英]ではby ship。a satisfied customer (よいお客) のこと。特にアメリカでは，このように自分を売り込んでよい。satisfied は excellent でも regular でもよい。I trust that ～ はI am sure that ～ よりも格式ばった表現。in your records「貴社の記録に」とは，コンピューターに記録されていることを意味する。

[Sample letter 20]

Dear Mr. Green:

Subject: Direct Shipment of Order #99-1008 to Okinawa

We enclose our Order No. 99-1008 for fifty Long-Lasting Hoses and ask that you ship the goods direct to the Zamami Kami Shoten, Okinawa.

Please charge them at $845.20 each FOB Leiden, and follow the instructions of our December 23, 1998 letter. (Please send the 30% commission to our bank.)

Finally, please send us by return airmail the contract drawn up in triplicate to the Zamami Kami Shoten in the form we have previously used.

We appreciate your best and prompt attention.

Yours faithfully,

【注】代理店契約をしているため，品物はオランダの工場から沖縄へ直納して，その手数料を日本の取扱銀行に払い込めという内容の手紙である。We enclose 〜「〜を同封しました」(77ページ参照)。Long-Lasting Hoses「耐久力のある[長持ちのする；丈夫な]ホース」。charge「勘定につける」

FOBは，F.O.B.; fob; f.o.b.とも書き，[ef ou bi:]と読む。free on board ([輸出港] 本船渡し [条件; 値段] のこと。CIFと共にもっとも代表的な貿易取引条件で，買主が手配した輸出港所在の本船へ荷物を積み込めば売主の義務は終わる。値段はそれまでの費用を含む。詳しくは119ページ参照。Leiden [láiden] オランダ南西部の港。commission「手数料」。by return airmail「折返しの航空便で」。contract「契約書」。drawn up in triplicate「3通に作成して(ある)」。

第9章 遅延状

　船積みの遅延 (delay in delivery) は，不可抗力 (force majeure) などの正当な理由がなければ契約違反になる。止むを得ない事情があるときは，証明できる書類を送ったり，説明をして相手を説得しなければならない。約束の納期に遅れる恐れが生じたら直ちに遅延状を出すべきである。注文が取消されるのではないか，相手が面倒な要求をしてくるのではないかのような心配をするあまり手紙を出すのが億劫になるものだが，いつかは書かねばならないのだから早いに越したことはない。

9.1　参考覚書

　遅延は，覚書に記載の条項に則り免責が受けられる。次のような覚書が参考になる。

　Shipment is to be made within the time stipulated in each contract, except in circumstances beyond Sellers' control. The date of Bills of Lading shall be taken as the conclusive proof of the date of shipment. Unless expressly agreed upon, the port of shipment shall be at Sellers' option. (船積みは，各契約で定められた期日以内に行うこと。ただし，売手にとっての不可抗力＜Force Majeure＞たる事情の発生した場合はこの限りでない。船荷証券の日付が，船積日の最終的証拠とみなされる。明確に打合せのない限り，船積港は売手の選択権とする。) ―石田貞夫:『貿易実務』(有斐閣ビジネス) pp. 118-119

9.2　内容構成

　遅延は一般に「船積遅延 (Delayed Shipment)」，「航海の遅延 (Delay in Voyage)」を指す。いずれにしても事実を説明し，どのような解決法を取ったのかを明記することが肝要である。手紙一本で解決できるか否かが

決まることが多いので、ビジネスマンの手腕はここにあるといえよう。

　We must *apologize for* not replying sooner to your letter. (ご返事が遅れて申し訳ございません) のように、We must apologize for ... は常套文。

9.3　例文

[Sample letter 21]

Attn: Mr. William A Cunningham

Re: Delay of Order No. 99-24

Gentlemen:

In reference to your Order No. 99-24 for 88 machines, which you forwarded to us on February 2, 20XX, we regret that due to a great influx of orders production facilities were overtaxed during this period. This caused a delay and created a backlog in our production schedule, since parts had to be manufactured to take care of the abnormal number of production orders received during this period.

However, you may recall that upon your inquiry, we faxed you on April 10, 20XX, indicating that all the machines on your order were duly shipped per SS "IVARAN," which left Yokohama on April 5. We also requested that you inspect and clear them upon arrival at San Francisco.

We trust that as of this date these machines have arrived safely and in perfect condition, and that you will be able to service your customers as the exclusive Shutters agent in the USA.

We regret any inconvenience the delay in production at our facilities may have caused you during this period.

Sincerely,

【注】この手紙は米国の代理店から，88台の機械を注文してあるが，遅れを催促されて，その遅延理由を報告した手紙である。実情を説明したあとで，解決したことを述べている。

In reference to は As for でも Regarding でもよい。forwarded to us = sent to us。a great influx of orders「大きい注文が流れ込む」influx は a sudden influx of imported personal computers on the market（輸入パソコンが突然に市場に流れ込む）のように使われる。overtax「過度な負担をうける」。create a backlog「受注残高を生じる」。take care of = deal with; fill; fulfill（を処理する）。you may recall ～「～を思い出すでしょう」丁重に相手に注意を喚起している。upon your inquiry「貴社から問い合わせを受けるや」。fax「ファックスをいれる」。per = by; on。per は古いので使用を戒めている参考書もある。SS "IVARAN"「IVARAN号」。船名。SS は steamship の略。S / S; S.S.; s / s; s.s.などと略記されるが，出航予定表（shipping schedule）に記載の通りに書く。ss の前に定冠詞を付ける人もいるが，per の次には付けないのが普通である。clear「通関する」。We trust ～ = We believe ～。as of this date「現在のところ」。as the exclusive ～ agent in the USA「米国における～の一手販売代理店」。inconvenience（ご不便）と the delay の間に関係代名詞を入れて考える。

[Sample letter 22]

Dear Mr. Lovell:

Subject: Delay of Orders T-99-2032 and E-99-2278

With reference to the above orders, we deeply apologize for our

delay in the delivery of the goods. They were late because of:
1. the manufacturer's two-week summer holiday.
2. the two-month delay in MITI's foreign exchange allocation.
3. the New York dockworker's strike.

However, the ship carrying the goods has now docked at Yokohama, and we are going through customs formalities. Delivery should be made by December 10, 20XX at the latest.

We hope you can appreciate the situation.

Yours sincerely,

【注】簡単な遅延状の例である。日本に駐在する外資系の機関から受注した注文品の納期が遅れたことをその機関に告げて，許可を求める手紙である。遅延した理由を明確に述べ，納品できる日を明記することが大切である。格式高く，丁重に書く。With reference to = As to; Concerning; In connection with。apologize (for; to) ~「~を謝る」。MITI は Ministry of International Trade and Industry (通商産業省) の略。foreign exchange allocation (外貨資金割当) 略してFA制という。dockworker は，従来は longshoreman (港湾労働者; 沖仲士) と言われたが，この語は -man を使っているため性差別語。docker; wharf-hand; stevedore が無難。「1.9 差別語を避ける」を参照。go through ~「~を通過する」。customs formalities「通関手続」。Delivery「納品」。at the latest「遅くとも」。[例] Please be here by 10 o'clock *at the latest*. (遅くとも10時までにはお出でください)

第10章 積出し

　成約後，買手は信用状や積出しに必要な書類を売手に送って約定品の到着を待つ。売手は商品の手配・船腹の予約 (booking of ship's space)・保険の手配 (arrangements for insurance)・通関 (customs clearance) などの手続きをする。船積み予定が立った段階で買手に出港予定日や船名を通知するが，契約品を積出した直後に，船積通知 [出荷案内] (Shipping Advice; Notice of Shipment) を買手に送ることになっている。これらの関係書類は書式の決まったものが多い。

　輸出地の銀行から支払を受けるには，信用状 (第11章参照)，D/P手形，D/A手形の何れの場合でも，為替手形 (Draft) に船積書類 (Shipping Documents) を添付した荷為替手形 (Documentary Draft) を銀行に提出する。

10.1　船積書類

　通常，FOB契約では，物品の引渡しを主眼とするため，運賃着払いの船荷証券 (Collect B/L) と送り状 (Invoice) が要求される。貿易取引でInvoiceというと，通常，商業送り状 (Commercial Invoice) をさす。Invoice は輸出入の通関手続きに必要となる重要な書類で，輸出者が作成する。運送貨物の明細書であり，輸出代金の請求書でもある。出荷案内書 (納品書) の役目も果たす。船荷証券 (Bill of Lading)，海上保険証券 (Marine Insurance Policy) と共に，主要な船積書類 (Shipping Documents) の一つである。船名，船積日，船積地，仕向港，品名，数量，単価，金額，荷印などの明細が書かれている。

　CIF契約では，書類の引渡しによる売買契約なので，運賃前払済み船荷証券 (Prepaid B/L) と送り状，海上保険証券 (Marine Insurance Policy) または承認状 (Certificate) が要求される。

10.2　船荷書類

船荷書類は次のようなもので構成されている。

　　船荷証券 (Bill of Lading; B/L)
　　保険証券または承認状 (Insurance Policy or Certificate)
　　商業送り状 (Commercial Invoice)
　　包装明細書 (Packing List)
　　容積重量証明書 (Certificate and List of Measurement and/or Weight)
　　領事送り状 (Consular Invoice)
　　税関送り状 (Customs Invoice)
　　検査証明書 (Inspection Certificate)
　　衛生証明書 (Health Certificate; Sanitary Certificate) など。

10.3　船荷証券

貨物を受取ったことを船会社が証明する受領書であり，貨物の引換証。また，運送契約の証拠であり，譲渡可能で (negotiable) 流通する。次のような種類がある。

　　船積船荷証券 (Shipped B/L)　　受取船荷証券 (Received B/L)
　　無故障船荷証券 (Clean B/L)　　故障船荷証券 (Foul B/L)
　　記名式船荷証券 (Straight B/L)　指図式船荷証券 (Order B/L)

船荷証券とは性質を異にするものに，航空貨物運送状 (Air Waybill) [流通性がない] (Not Negotiable)，郵便小包受領証 (Parcel Post Receipt) [流通性がない]，船積小荷物受領証 (Shipping Parcel Receipt) [流通性がない] などがある。

10.4　海上保険

CIFでは，保険料 (premium) が含まれているので輸出者が支払う。FOB や CFR (C & F) では，輸入者が自分の費用で手配する。しかし，輸出者が輸入者に代わって手配することがある。国際商業会議所が新しくコード化するに際し，&が使えなくなったため Cost & Freight の

略称として CFR とした。

　保険では損害填補の範囲を明確にする必要がある。

　海上損害 (Marine Loss) は，全損 (Total Loss) と分損 (Partial Loss) に大別される。全損には現実全損 (Actual Total Loss) と推定全損 (Constructive Total Loss) があり，分損には共同海損 (General Average) と単独海損 (Particular Average) がある。

10.5　航空貨物

　航空貨物の場合は，全損になることが予想されるので保険条件は全危険担保 (All Risks) となるのが一般的で，ICC (Air) (excluding sending by post) が適用される。なお，ICC (Air) は Institute Cargo Clauses の略称で「協会貨物約款（航空）」として，ロンドン保険協会が作成したもの。

10.6　貿易条件

　売手と買手の費用負担と上に略記した危険負担の範囲を規定することが貿易取引の基本である。ここでは，代表的な輸送条件を述べる。
（1）Ex Factory「工場渡し価格」。商品を製造した場所で引渡す条件で国内取引で用いる。危険負担と運賃・保険料の負担売手なし。
（2）Ex Godown「指定倉庫渡し価格」。輸出者が指定した場所で引渡しをする条件で国内取引で用いる。Ex Warehouseともいう。危険負担と運賃・保険料の負担売手なし。
（3）FAS (Free Alongside Shipの略）。「輸出港船側渡し価格」。売手は，買手が指定する船舶の船側で，貨物を買手に渡す条件。積出港まで売手に責任。危険負担と運賃・保険料は買手の負担。
（4）FOB (Free On Boardの略)「本船渡し価格」。輸出港の本船に貨物を積込んだ段階で引渡す条件。FOB Airport (空港渡し) もある。売手の負担は輸出港の本船上で終了。運賃・保険料は買手の負担。
（5）CFR (C & F) [Cost and Freightの略]。「運賃込み価格」「FOB +

仕向港までの運送費込み価格」。売手の負担は輸出港の本船上で終了。運賃は売手，保険料は買手の負担。
（6）CIF (Cost, Insurance and Freightの略)。「運賃・保険料込み価格」。「C & F +「仕向港までの保険料込み価格」。売手の負担は輸出港の本船上で終了。運賃・保険料は売手の負担。

（2）から（6）までは，FOB Yokohama のように，港名か空港名を付けるだけでよい。
（7）Freight / Carriage Paid to「運賃支払済み」
（8）Freight / Carriage and Insurance Paid to「運賃保険料支払済み」
この章の詳しくは貿易実務書で学ぶこと。

10.7 例文

[Sample letter 23]

Dear Mr. Wells:

Thank you very much for your order of September 15 for heavy-duty Cellular Phone GT2000. Enclosed is our confirmation.

The equipment will soon be ready for shipment and we have made tentative arrangements to effect shipment of this order by M/S "Heiwa Maru" leaving here for New York on September 20. However, your L/C to cover this order has not reached us as yet. Therefore, please contact your supplier, urging them to arrange to open it as quickly as possible, if it is not opened yet.

Thanks again for your order.

Sincerely,

【注】「your order of + 日付 for + 品物」の構文に注意。「your order of + 品物 of + 日付」の構文では of が品物を修飾してしまうので不可。heavy-duty「頑丈な」。Enclosed is our confirmation. は We enclose our confirmation. (当社は注文確認書を同封いたしました)。tentative arrangements「仮予約; 仮手配」。to effect shipment of this order は to ship this order (この注文品を船積みする) より格式ばった表現。by the M / S "Heiwa Maru"「平和丸号で」。船名はダブルクォーテイションマークで囲むことが多い。M / S は M.S.; m / s; m.s. と略され motorship のこと。ほかに S / S; s/s; s.s. もある。これは steamship の略。M/V; M.V.; m / v; m.v. は motor vessel の略。いずれを使うかは, sailing schedule (出港予定表) に書いてある通りがよい。per s.s. "Heiwa Maru"も「平和丸で」のことだが 通例 per のときは冠詞は付けない。per a cent と言わないことからも理解できよう。leaving は which will leave のこと。urging them = asking them のこと。この them は the supplier を指す。

[Sample letter 24]

Dear Mr. Dearing:

We have just received the L/C covering your order NO. 20-1234. Thank you very much.

We faxed you on August 15, as per copy enclosed, asking you to extend the validity and shipment time of the L/C to the end of this month. This was because there was a strike in the plant that was making your products. This is a case of *force majeure*. So, we ask you to please understand the circumstances and comply with our request.

We are pleased to inform you that the products will be shipped during November.

Sincerely,

【注】信用状の内容の変更を申し出た書状である。covering は which covers のこと。Thank you very much の次に for opening the credit（信用状を開設していただき）を続ける必要はない。直前で the L/C といっているので。faxed「ファックスいたしました」。fax は動詞で使ってよい。as per copy enclosed は as per enclosed copy と同じ。as per を使うのを非難しているアメリカの参考書もある。as shown in the enclosed copyが無難。as per = according to。to extend the validity and shipment time of the L/C to ～「信用状の有効期限と船積日を～まで延ばす」validity の代わりに expiry も使われる。*force majeure* [fɔːrs máːdʒəː]。「不可抗力」輸出者の不手際や怠慢による契約違反は重大なクレームの対象になるが，台風や地震のような天災，ストや革命などの場合は，その対象にならないのが普通。契約書を作成のときに一般取引条件して協定しておくとよい。circumstances「状況」。comply with ～ = follow; obey「～に応じる」[例] The factory was closed for failing to *comply with* government safety regulations. ―LDCE（政府の安全規則に応じられなくて工場は閉鎖した）。during November「11月中」と安全さを考えて during で申し出ている。

[Sample letter 25]

Dear Mr. Mallory:

We are pleased to inform you that your Order No. 20-2345 was shipped on July 1 on board the S.S. "Heian Maru" leaving Kobe for your destination.

We enclose a nonnegotiable copy of B/L and copies of Insurance Policy, Invoice, and Packing List.

We trust that the documents will be found in order, and that the goods will reach you in good condition.

Sincerely,

【注】ルーティーン化した書状の例といえる。輸出者は契約品が実際に積出された時点に積出通知 (Shipping Advice) を輸入者に送付するのが義務といえる。ship「積出す」は船積みだけではなく，航空機，鉄道などの手段にも用いられる。leaving は which leaves のこと。destination「仕向地」。nonnegotiable「譲渡できない」。We trust that 〜 はWe are sure that 〜 より格式ばった表現。trust の代わりに believe でもよい。in good condition は in good order でもよいが，すぐ前に order があるので condition とした。

第11章

支払い

　貿易取引の支払い (payment) は，荷為替手形や送金 (remittance) などにより銀行を利用する方法が主である。

11.1　手形の種類

　荷為替手形には支払渡し手形 (Documents against Payment; 略称 D/P) と引受渡し手形 (Documents against Acceptance; 略称 D/A) がある。

　D/P 手形決済では，輸出者振出しの荷為替手形 (Documentary Bill of Exchange; Documentary Draft) を輸入地の銀行で提示された時点で，輸入者が支払いを済ました段階で船積書類が入手でき，輸入品が引取れる。輸入者は，期限付き D/P 手形では満期日前に支払わない限り，品物の引取りが手形の満期日まで延ばされるので，輸入者に不利である。

　D/A手形では，輸入者が手形の引受けさえすれば，手形代金の支払いなしに船積書類が入手できるので，輸入者は自己資金を利用しないで輸入貨物の引取り，売買ができる。したがって輸入者にとって有利である。

11.2　支払い時期

支払いの時期には次の5つの種類がある。

（1）本船受取証 (mate's receipt; 略称M/R)・運送書類 (Transport Documents) の証書など契約品の出荷証明書を輸出地にある輸入者の支店か銀行に渡し，それと引替えに輸出者が支払いを受ける方法 (Cash on Shipment)
（2）輸出者の支店が輸入者の土地に存在する場合，その支店が取引している銀行に支払う方法
（3）荷為替手形を買取る荷為替 (Documentary Bill; Documentary Draft) による方法。最も一般的な方法

（4）買い主が契約品を受取った後，送金為替 (mail remittance) による後払い法 (deferred payment)

（5）注文払い (Cash with Order) に見られるように，送金為替による前払い法 (Payment in Advance)

　広く用いられてきた決済方法の一つは信用状 (Letter of Credit; 略称 L/C) による。信用状とは，輸入者の依頼で，輸入者の取引銀行が発行する支払保証書である。輸出者は注文品の積出し終了後，船荷書類 (Shipping Documents) を添えて為替手形 (Bill of Exchange; 略称 draft) を振り出し，それを銀行に買い取って (negotiate) もらって輸出代金を入手する。このとき，輸入者から送られてきた信用状があると支払いが保証されたことになるので，銀行は安心して買取ってくれる。

　輸入者がその取引銀行に L/C の発行を依頼する銀行を開設（または発行）銀行 (Opening Bank; Issuing Bank; Establishing Bank) といい，輸出者が通知する銀行を通知銀行 (Advising Bank; Notifying Bank) という。開設銀行から輸出者へ直接送付されるか，輸出者の取引銀行 (Correspondent Bank) を径由して輸出者へ通知されるからである。

　信用状は，発行銀行が，輸入者のために輸出者に対して船積書類を添付した為替手形 (Documentary Bill of Exchange)，すなわち，船荷書類の添付された為替手形なので荷為替信用状 (Documentary Letter of Credit; Documentary Credit) ともいう。

　L/Cに記載通りの船積書類を銀行に提出しなければ，銀行は買取ってくれないから輸出者はL/Cを入手したら，記載事項を確実にチェックしなければならない。

11.3　信用状の種類

　信用状には，Irrevocable L/C「取消不能信用状」，Revocable L/C「取消し可能信用状」，Confirmed L/C「確認信用状」，Transferable L/C「譲渡可能信用状」などがある。

(1) Irrevocable L/C

　　輸出者は，L/Cを入手したが，船積手配中にL/Cを取り消された

ら大きい損害を被ることになる。従って，輸出者は，有効期間中は，発行銀行・確認銀行および受益者 (Beneficiary) の同意が一方的に変更や取消しができないので，取消不能信用状を必ず要求すべきである。Irrevocable と明示するべきだが，明示がないと取消不能として取扱われる。取消可能の場合には，必ず Revocable の表示がなされていなければならない。輸入者である買い手は売買契約が成立した後，L/C 決済の場合は直ぐに輸出者である売り手を受益者として取消不能信用状を開設しなければならない。

(2) Revocable L/C

L/C を受取っても，船積手配をしていても，手形買取り前であれば，いつでも取消すことができる。

(3) Confirmed L/C

信用状の発行銀行以外の銀行が，発行銀行と同じ支払い保証をしている信用状。輸出者が発行銀行だけの支払いで安心でき，別の銀行の保証を輸入者に求める理由がないのであれば無確認信用状 (Unconfirmed L/C)，すなわち，取消不能信用状となる。

(4) Transferable L/C

L/C の受益者が，その金額の一部か全部を第3者に譲渡することを許すものだが，譲渡された者が更に第3者に譲渡することはできない。

11.4　簡単な取立状

近ごろは海外でも容易にクレジットカードで買い物ができるため，取り立てで苦労することが生じている。簡単な取立状では，次の点に注意をするとよい。

* 取立状に請求書の写しを同封する。
* 取り立てることが先決であり，相手はお客様であることを忘れないこと。最初の手紙から相手を責めないように注意しよう。
* 第一パラグラフで買って貰った製品に満足していただいていることを書く。
   I hope that your computer is performing according to your expectations.

(お買い上げのコンピューターはご期待通りに作動しているものと思います)

＊ 第二パラグラフで未払いの状況を説明し，請求金額を書く。

As you can see from the enclosed statement, we have not received payment for the ～. The balance due is $500. (同封の明細からお分かりのように，～に対して，未払になっております。残高は500ドルです)

ここでは，信用状の送付を輸入者にお願いする例と，信用状の内容に変更が生じた場合に起こる信用状の訂正に対する例文を検討してみよう。

11.5　例文

[Sample Letter 26]

Dear Mr. Kern:

<u>Asking Payment</u>

A recent review of your account indicates that as of January 15, 20xx, we had not received the amount due of $80.00.

If you have not already paid this amount, please either mail us your check or money order for the amount due or pay it at your local Evergreen store. This is essential in order to maintain a current status on your account. If payment has been made, please accept our thanks.

As a major credit grantor, we report the way all credit accounts are paid to credit bureaus each month. Paying the amount due will allow us to continue to report your account as current.

Please be assured that you are a valued customer at Evergreen. If you have any questions concerning your account, please contact us at the address or telephone number shown.

    Phone: (800) 537-5591

Sincerely,

Yoshio Nagano
Account Representative

【注】物品を購入する際にクレジットカードなどを使って支払いを済ませたが, 取扱い銀行が決済してくれないケースに対しての購入者への取立状である。第一パラグラフで事情と金額を説明している。review = inspection。account「勘定書; 請求書」。as of 〜「〜のところ」は法律用語。As of May 15, 20XX, this contract becomes effective. (20XX年5月15日よりこの契約は効力を発する)。the amount due of $80.00「当然支払うべき80ドルという金額」。

  第二パラグラフは仮定法を使って丁重にお願いをしながら, この手紙の目的を述べている。money order「(郵便) 為替」。[英] postal order。local「近くの」。current status「現在の地位」。accept our thanks は「当社の感謝を受け入れて下さい」, つまり「御礼申し上げます」のこと。Please *accept our thanks* for all your help. (あなたのご援助に御礼申し上げます)。

  第三パラグラフでは不払いの場合を客観的に, 丁重に説明している。a major credit grantor (一流の信用譲与会社) とは自社, つまり Evergreen store をさす。credit account「掛け売り (勘定)」charge account ともいう。credit bureau「商業興信所」。allow = permit。Paying the amount due 〜 as current. の文は, If you pay the amount due, we will continue to report your account as current. のこと。

  第四パラグラフでは丁重な結び文になっている。Please be assured that 〜. は You may be sure that 〜. の丁重な表現。手紙の本文に address が書かれていないのは, この letter paper に Letterhead が印刷されているため。

[Sample letter 27]

Dear Mr. Kaufman:

Subject: Issuance of invoices for LGP 30 Computer

We have received your letter of April 1 concerning the invoice for shipment of LGP 30 from the U.S.A., and are sorry for the delay in answering. Please note that after shipment a delay of 2-3 weeks in the issuing of the invoice is unavoidable. In order to avoid problems caused by licensing and customs clearance, we ask you to please follow the invoice procedure outlined below in this and future orders of the Computer, Printers, OCRs, and their software.

1. As soon as freight charges are decided after shipment, please airmail us from Holland the Proforma Invoice on the CFR Yokohama basis. According to this, we will go through the temporary customs regulations after obtaining our banker's certificate.
2. Please issue two separate invoices from the main office as follows:

   Invoice 1: as stated above on the CFR basis of the same value at the said Proforma Invoice of Holland; send it to us by airmail through the bank. Following this, we will go through the formal customs regulations.

   Invoice 2: covering all the other expenses excepting the CFR amount; send it direct to us, not through the bank. These additional charges will be deducted from our credit account for settlement.

第11章　支払い

We are sorry for the delay and thank you for your prompt attention.

Sincerely,

【注】信用状の発行をお願いする手紙である。
　　　invoice「送り状；インボイス」。LGP 30 はコンピューターの機種名。We have received が普通で，We are in receipt of は古い言い方。your letter of April 1 は your April 1 letter が多用されるようになっている。concerning は格式語で on か about でよい。Please note that ...「that の以下のことにお気付き下さい」のことだが，注意を喚起するのに用いている。after shipment「出荷後」。
　　　licensing ([政府の] 許可を得る)。貿易には輸出承認 (Export License: E/L) か輸入承認 (Import License: I/L) を政府から得なければならない。経済産業省 (METI) に申請して承認を得る。License は経済産業省から得る「(事前) 承認 (書)」のことで，Permit は税関からの「許可 (書)」をいう。
　　　customs clearance「出港許可書」。海外の港に向けて出港するとき，税関に提出する出港届。
　　　procedure「手続き」。OCR = optical character reader「光学読取装置」。freight charge「運送費用；輸送費用」
　　　Proforma Invoice「見積り送り状; 試算用送り状; 仮送り状; プロフォーマ」。商業送り状の一種で，売買契約が締結する前に，輸入者に対して輸出者が，将来取引きが締結され，船積みされる場合を予想して作成する送り状。輸入申請をする際の添付書類として利用するほか，輸入しようとする品物の輸入価格を計算するのに利用する。
　　　on the CFR Yokohama basis「横浜港運賃込み渡しで」。CFR に保険料 (Insurance) を加算すると C.I.F. (運賃・保険料込み渡し) になる。According to this は Based on this でもよい。
　　　go through「を終える; をふむ」。regulations「(税関) 諸規則」。deduct「を控除する」。credit account「掛け勘定」。settlement「決済; 清算」。

[Sample letter 28]

Dear Ms. Shudian,

Subject: <u>Shipment of Order # 2124</u>

As per our letter of March 13 (our ref. No. 2124), we are pleased to inform you that the 2,000 copies of books on your order in 600 packages amounting to £4.000 have just been shipped to you by surface at book rate. We enclose the invoice.

We are also very happy to confirm that we have just received an advance from your bankers showing the adjustment by £4.000 of the value of your L/C and extending the validity to April 30, 20xx.

The next shipment of books on your order, amounting to about £500, is to be shipped by ocean freight as noted in our letter of March 31. This shipment will fill your current order. We would be pleased to be of assistance in any future orders you may have.

We would like to inform you that we have succeeded in securing the following two books for you at the prices quoted below:

  JM2 - 6444 - 4648 ¥30,000 less 10% ¥27,000.
  JM2 - 6259 - 69   ¥60,000 less 10% ¥54,000.

We would be pleased to supply you with these books as soon as we receive your confirmation of order.

                Very truly yours,

第11章　支払い

【注】our ref. No. = our reference number (当社の参照番号)。we are pleased to inform you 〜 については「1.2 Softener が大切」を参照。book rate「書籍料金」米では 4th class mail という。We are also very happy to confirm that 〜「〜ということを確認いたします」。We are very happy to 〜 については「1.2 Softener が大切」を参照。advance「前払い；立替金」。bankers「取引銀行」。英国系では bankers と一銀行であっても複数形にすることがあり，米では bank と単数形で書く傾向が強い。showing は stating でもよい。adjustment「精算」。extending the validity to 〜「〜まで有効期間を延ばす」「有効期間」は term of validity が普通。by ocean freight「海洋運賃で」(陸運賃に対して)。fill your current order「貴社の最近のご注文に応じる」。We would be 〜 you may have. は追加注文を催促した巧妙な言い方。secure = get as the result of effort。less はここでは前置詞で「を減じた；を引いた」。supply 〜 with の構文に注意。confirmation of order「注文確認書」。

第12章 クレーム

　貿易取引上で起こる損害賠償請求をクレーム (claim) という。Claim とは「権利の主張」を意味し，compensation (求償) [英] ともいう。クレームにならない complaint (苦情) もある。

12.1 発生するケース

　クレームには様々なケースがある。

(1) 品質不良 (inferior quality)
(2) 品違い (wrong article)
(3) 品質相違 (different quality)
(4) 貨物の損傷 (damaged goods)
(5) 船積遅延 (delayed shipment)
(6) 船積不履行 (non-delivery; non-shipment)
(7) 船積相違 (different shipment)
(8) 数量・個数不足 (shortage)
(9) 包装不備 (bad packing)
(10) 法規違反 (illegal shipment)
(11) 契約不履行 (breach of contract)
(12) 解約 (cancellation)
(13) マーケット・クレーム (market claim)

　メーカーは自社が製造した製品を限られた期間内保証する義務がある。製造物責任 (products liability [PLは和製英語])といい，製品やマニュアルに注意の表示を明示することが法律で定められている。これを怠って，ユーザーが怪我をしたり，機械が頻繁に故障するとユーザーはメーカーを訴えることがある。

　従って，このような事故を防ぐために，品物やマニュアルに明示し

てある事項を実行しないとユーザーが死か重傷につながる可能性が99%の場合は DANGER（赤）と，50%ぐらいなら WARNING（オレンジ色）と，軽傷を負う可能性がある場合は CAUTION（黄）とメーカーが明示することが義務づけられている。機械やプログラム，システムなどの損傷についても同様の表示が適用される。

12.2　対処法

　クレームが生じたら，迅速・慎重に処理し，できる限り話し合いで和解 (compromise; amicable settlement) するように努めるべきである。解決方法として，和解，斡旋 (conciliation)，仲裁 (arbitration)，訴訟 (suit) などがある。天災や天候不良・不作・革命・ストライキのような不可抗力 (*force majeure*) による場合は，直ちに原因を買い手に通知して，クレームに発展しないように努めるべきである。

　文章は，感情に走らず，事実を明記し，実施した調査を述べ，解決案も具体的に述べて，取引関係を損なわないようにすることが肝要である。

12.3　内容構成

12.3.1　苦情の手紙

次の内容でまとめるとよい。
* 状況を時間順に説明する。
* 製品名，日時，注文番号，Invoice 番号なども明記する。
* 解決法を書く。
* 相手を決して責めない。こちらの希望通りに解決して貰うように努力する。

12.3.2　苦情への返事

次の手順で書くのがよいだろう。
* 簡単な謝罪か手紙をいただいたお礼から始める。

　Thank you for your letter of September 13. I was sorry to hear of the difficulties you were having with your Personal Computer.（9月13日付けお手紙有り難うございましいた。ご使用中のパソコンの具合が悪いとの

こと残念に存じます）
第二パラグラフで相手が満足すると思えるような解決法を述べる。
第三パラグラフで原因を簡単に説明する。
第四パラグラフで今後のビジネス関係の持続をお願いする。

　Please accept my sincere apology for the confusion.　Please let me know if I can be of any further help.（ご迷惑をお掛けし，心からお詫びいたします。お役に立てることがございましたらお申しつけください）

12.4　例文

[Sample letter 29]

Dear Mr. Monroe:

　　Subject: <u>Damage Claim for Monroe Calculating Machine</u>

　We hereby file a claim for damage to an Electric Calculator crushed by pressure.　This item was carried by the s.s. Kamikawa Maru (B/L Permit No. FMB 717), which arrived on March 18, 19xx in Yokohama from New York.
　The details and the amount of the claim are as follows:
　1. Case No. 90.　Machine No. 617428
　　　Monroe Calculating Machine (66N-213)
　　　Absolute total loss
　　　CFR $645.98・・・(￥130：US$1.00)・・・￥83,977.00
　We request that you investigate the matter immediately, and compensation at your earliest convenience will be highly appreciated.

Yours faithfully,

【注】hereby「ここに」は格式ばった語で法律文で多用される。file a claim「クレームを提起する」。damage では曖昧なので明確に crushed by pressure (圧力によって押しつぶされた) と説明している。B / L = bill of lading (船荷証券) [b.l. ともB.L. とも略す]。total loss「全損」。CFR = Cost and Freight「運賃込み値段」。(￥130: US$1.00) は exchange rate, one hundred thirty yen to US one dollar のこと。We request (を要請する) は We ask より堅い。compensation「補償」。at your earliest convenience「ご都合つき次第」。

[Sample letter 30]

Dear Mr. Franklin:

Subject: <u>Amendment to Invoice No. 99-6288</u>

At the time of arrival at Narita Airport, Invoice No. 99-6288, upon inspection by a customs officer, was found to contain discrepancies. The number of parts recorded on the invoice did not match the number of parts included in the shipment. Because of this, we were not permitted to take delivery of the shipment. Please see below:

Q'ty specified in Invoice		Actually shipped q'ty
Interchange parts	1625	1655
Navigator parts	5	3

We would appreciate it if you would airmail us a revised invoice covering the actual quantities of parts supplied. (Please specify therein "No Charge". For the convenience of clearing customs, there is no need for the extra parts to change the invoice value at this time.

The inspection by customs has been especially strict as of late. In the future, too, please be more careful to match the numbers specified in the invoice with the numbers included in shipment.

We would appreciate your cooperation in this matter.

Sincerely,

【注】 upon inspection「検査のとき」。discrepancy = difference; lack of agreement。shipment はここでは「積送品」のこと。take delivery「引き渡す」。Q'ty = quantity。revised invoice「修正した送り状」。therein (in that place) は堅い語だから使用を戒めている参考書もある。"No Charge"「無料」。value「金額; 価格」。at this time「今回は」。For the convenience of ～「～の利便を考えて」。clearing customs「通関する」。as of late = recently。match ～ withの構文に注意。in this matter「本件に」。

第13章

各種英文書

13.1　開店披露状

　この種の手紙は，いつ (when)，何を (what)，どこで (where) 始めるかを明記しなければならない。会社の宣伝も忘れてはならない。

[Sample Letter 31]

Ladies and Gentlemen:

Subject: Opening of our new facility

We are pleased to announce to all our customers the opening of a new facility here at 23 Polar Street, South Rutherford, New Jersey. This home office will supply our branches in the United States as well as all our customers and distributors throughout the world.

Our new facility includes: the nation's largest selection of computers; a rebuilding plant for office machines, parts and accessories; and a plant for rubber platens. Please find herewith our wholesale price list which covers the selection of used computers, including rental grade and rebuilt.

We wish to call your particular attention to our IBM computers, rebuilt in our modern plant and painted in gray, tan, green and blue cascade.

Shipman Ward has been serving office machine dealers throughout the world for nearly 70 years. The combination of experience, large stocks of machines, and modern facilities place this company in the number one position among the most important office machine suppliers in this country.

We hope to receive your esteemed orders.

Sincerely,

Takeo Ando
Export Manager

【注】冒頭文は，この種の手紙で多用される英文。We are pleased to ～ は We are happy to ～ より格式張った表現。It is our great pleasure to ～ は更に格式張った表現になる。1.1「大切な語調」を参照。home office = head office; main office (本社)。branch (es)「支店」。supply our branches in the United States ～ は supply our United States branches with office machines ～ のこと [米では with が省略されることがある]。the nation's largest selection of computers「アメリカで最も多くコンピューターを精選」。rebuilding「(古い機械を新しく)組立て直す」。accessories「付属品」。a factory for rubber platens は a rubber platen factory「ゴム製のプラテン (を作る) 工場」。find herewith は find with this, つまり We enclose in this letter ～. のこと。wholesale price list「卸売値段表」。rental grade「レンタル品」。rebuilt = rebuilt machines。We wish to ～ は We want to ～ や We would like to ～ より丁寧な表現。call your attention to ～「～に注意を引いて (いただきたい)」。blue cascade「青の滝状のレース」。place は put より格式張った動詞で「(第一位) に入れている[考えている]」。We hope to ～ orders. は Hoping to receive your esteemed orders, we are では古く，堅い表現といわれている。your esteemed orders「(あなた様の) ご注文」cf. your esteemed letter (お手紙; 貴信)。

13.2　お礼状

ここでは，簡単で，短いお礼状から長いお礼状へと，その例を紹介していく。お礼状を書くときの要点は，感謝の気持ちを丁重に表すべきだが，その他に，楽しかったこと，有益だったこと，記憶に残ったことなどを最低一つは挙げるべきだろう。

[Sample Letter 32]

Dear Mr. Smith:

Please accept this short note of thanks for your assistance and friendship during my recent stay in the U.S.

I hope that our association will be a lasting one; and that time and events will permit us to build on the friendship that we have established.

With cordial wishes for this new year, I am,

Sincerely yours,

> 【注】滞在中に受けた親切や恩恵に対する，ごく簡単なお礼状である。この種の形式的な手紙は bread and butter letter といわれている。short note「(形式ばらない) 短い手紙」。short はなくてもよい。I hope 以下はなくてもよい。付け足しである。association「関係，交際 (friendship)」。time and events will permit us to build on ～．「時間といろいろな事柄が私たちの友情に築かれるでしょう」とは「将来，友情が更に深まるでしょう」のこと。
> 　　With cordial wishes for ～new year, I am, は With cordial wishes for ～new year, I am sincerely yours, のことで旧式。

[Sample letter 33]

Dear Mr. Fisher:

I wanted to thank you for your warm hospitality on November 10, 20XX during my visit to New York. I very much enjoyed our dinner with Mr. Vlachos and also the time we spent at the Karaoke bar. I need to practice my singing before returning to the U.S. next year.

I hope that you have a healthy, happy and prosperous New Year. I look forward to seeing you next summer in Tokyo.

Sincerely,

【注】短い訪問中に受けた歓待に対する簡単なお礼状である。冒頭のI wanted to thank you for ～ は決り文句。楽しかったことを I very much enjoyed ～ で明記していることに注意。I hope that you have a healthy, happy and prosperous New Year.（新しい年のご健康とご多幸とご繁栄を祈念します）は I wish you and your family have a healthy, happy and prosperous New Year. でもよい。英米では３つ挙げる習慣がある。

[Sample Letter 34]

Dear Dean Kerr:

I want formally to thank you, your administration, faculty and students, for the wonderful welcome I enjoyed at ABC University during this past spring and summer while I served as a Visiting Professor in the School of Commerce.

I left New York with many happy memories, but foremost among them was the warm and generous reception I was accorded at ABC. I was impressed by the international spirit of your university and the open atmosphere of inquiry and intellectual activity among both faculty and students with whom I worked.

If there is some small way I can return the reception I received by serving as a point of contact between our universities, I will be happy to do so. Again I thank you for helping to provide me with the opportunity to enjoy a most memorable experience.

Sincerely yours,

【注】 administration はここでは「大学の本部」のこと。faculty「学部の先生（教授）方」。Visiting Professor「客員教授」。School of Commerce「商学部」。foremost among them「多くの中で先ずいちばんは」。accorded = given。open atmosphere「率直で開放的な空気」。inquiry「調査研究」。a most memorable experience「非常に記憶に残る経験」。

[Sample Letter 35]

Dear Mr. Gray:

Thank you for the many kindnesses and courtesies you extended to our members studying the Conveyor System.

They learned much during their months in the seminar at your firm and I feel their study will aid the further development of our system. They appreciated it very much.

Our new members will be visiting your firm around the beginning of March. We'll let you know the exact date when it is decided.

Please give my best regards to Mr. J.C. Proshan and his associates.

Sincerely,

Takeshi Saitoh
Manager, Export Department

【注】部下が滞在中にお世話になったお礼状である。この種の礼状では、どんな点に感銘を受けたかを明記すること。kindnesses and courtesies「ご親切やご好意」。Conveyor System「ベルトコンベーヤ」。firm「会社」。further development「今後の開発」。will be visiting ~「~を訪問する予定である」。will visitよりも確定的」。We'll let you know ~ は We'll inform you of ~ よりも口語的。Please give my best regards to ~ [Say hello to ~ は略式]「~に宜しくお伝えください」。regardsは常に複数形。associates「同僚」(colleague; co-worker)。

[Sample letter 36]

Dear Manager:

My position as office director is very rapidly drawing to a close. I have received a transfer paper on March 28 to the Public Relations Department in the Tokyo office as coordinator.

I will be leaving Washington on May 15, 2000. I am looking forward to the new assignment since it should prove interesting, challenging, and rewarding.

I have enjoyed a wonderful three years in Washington. I will never forget the beautiful scenery of the City or the warm, friendly, and industrious American people. I hope to return someday to Washington for either business or a nice long vacation.

Prior to leaving, I would like to take the opportunity to tell you that I have enjoyed my relations with you during the past 2 1/2 years. I very much appreciate the helpful, cooperative, and cheerful attitude which your personnel have exhibited in doing business with my office. The attitude displayed by your personnel has made my job easier and more pleasant.

Allow me to extend a most sincere "Thank you" and "Good bye" to all of your personnel who have been so helpful to me in the accomplishment of my work. I have thoroughly enjoyed my association with all of them.

Mr. Satoru Ishibashi will replace me as office director beginning

April 15. I hope the director will remain as efficient as always in business relations.

With best wishes,

Sincerely,

【注】外国勤務が解かれ，帰国に際してお世話になった客先の会社に出すお礼状である。「友好関係に感謝をし，滞在地を褒め，後任の氏名を書いて，私同様にお願いします」で結ぶのが普通である。position as office director「事務局長としての役職」。draw to a close「終わりに近づく」。ここでは「あと数日となる」こと。The meeting *drew into a close* at six. (会は6時に終わった)。I have received (a transfer paper on March 28)は，on March 28と日付けを表す副詞句を用いているが，現在完了形を使っている。学校文法には反するがこのような用法もある。a transfer paper「転勤通知状」。Public Relations Department「広報部」。coordinator「責任者；コーディネーター」。I am looking forward to ~「私は~を楽しみにしています」進行形は強調。toの後は名詞か動名詞。assignment「任務；仕事 (duty)」。challenging, and rewarding「魅力があり、やりがいがある」。take the opportunity to~「この機会を利用して~する」I'd like to *take this opportunity to* thank you for the hard work. (この機会を利用して，大変お骨折りをお掛けしたあなたに厚くお礼を述べたい)。 exhibited = showed。in doing business with my office「当社と仕事をするときに」。office は「会社；仕事をしている場所；執務室」と訳すときが多い。He's gone to the *office*. (彼は会社へ行きました)。 Allow me to extend ~ = I'd like to extend ~。略式では Let me explain ~。replace me as ~「~として私に代わる」Mr. Shimada has *replaced* Mr. Soeda as president of the company. (添田に代わって島田が社長になりました)。

13.3 ファクシミリの英語

ファクシミリの登場により電報やテレックスが影をひそめてしまった。電報やテレックスで使われる英語には独特のスタイルと特長があったが，ファクシミリで使われる英語は，手紙であれば手紙のスタイルや様式とほとんど同じである。しかしビジネスで未知の人にいきなりファクシミリで送信することはほとんどなく，国の内外の支社や傍系会社，あるいは同一社内，知人，友人に限られ，メモ的な報告から短い略式の手紙が多い。

一枚の Cover Sheet だけで終える場合もあれば数枚続けることもある。

13.3.1 カバーシートの例

カバーシート (Cover Sheet) には決まりはないが書かなければならない要素はある［Sample 37 参照］。

[Sample 37]

VIA FAX

To: Name	**From:** Name
Company Name	Company Name
Department	Department
Fax: Fax Number	**Fax:** Fax Number

Date:

　　　Number of sheets (including cover sheet):_____

Comments: _____
_____
_____
_____

If this fax reaches you in error, please forward it to the number above or contact sender. We appreciate it! (このファクスが誤送信でしたら，上記の番号にご転送下さるか，発信者へご連絡下さい。感謝いたします)

　【注】発信者の署名は，From にタイプされた人が，その名前の後に initial　　　　である。Salutation や Closing は省略することが多い。

[Sample 38]

facsimile
transmission

To: ＿＿＿＿＿＿＿＿
Fax #: ＿＿＿＿＿＿＿＿
Date: ＿＿＿＿＿＿＿＿
Subject: ＿＿＿＿＿＿＿＿＿＿＿＿＿＿＿＿＿
Pages: Number, including this cover sheet:＿＿＿

Comments:＿＿＿＿＿＿＿＿＿＿＿＿＿＿＿＿＿＿＿＿
＿＿＿＿＿＿＿＿＿＿＿＿＿＿＿＿＿＿＿＿＿＿＿＿
＿＿＿＿＿＿＿＿＿＿＿＿＿＿＿＿＿＿＿＿＿＿＿＿
＿＿＿＿＿＿＿＿＿＿＿＿＿＿＿＿＿＿＿＿＿＿＿＿
＿＿＿＿＿＿＿＿＿＿＿＿＿＿＿＿＿＿＿＿＿＿＿＿

If this fax reaches you in error, please forward it to the number above or contact sender. We appreciate it!

From the desk of ＿＿＿Name,＿＿＿Title＿＿＿＿＿＿＿
　　　　　　　(Company Name)
　　　　　　　(Address)
　　　　　Fax: (＿＿＿＿＿＿)

【注】発信者の署名は，From the desk of の後にタイプされた人が，その名前の後に initial でする。

13.3.2　ファックス通信文の例
[Sample 39]

Dumont Book Store
333 S. State St.
Ann Arbor, MI 444-56789
734/345-7653
FAX 734/345-2455

DATE: <u>September 2, 20xx</u>
DESTINATION:　<u>Yoshiaki Shinoda</u>
　　　　　　　<u>FAX: 087-345-678-8888</u>
ATTENTION: _____

This cover sheet is being followed by __0__ pages of transmission.

Message pertaining to this transmission: _____
<u>Here is the information on the books you inquired about:</u>
<u>"The ABC Communication" by Fear has been out of print since 1985. The publisher of "Process of Thought in Composition" seems to have gone out of business. I have written to their previous address and will contcat you.</u>
<u>Sorry not to be able to help.</u>

Please contact the person named below if there is a problem with the transmission:

Name: Alison Jones_____

Department: Special Order Dept._____

> 【注】DESTINATION「宛先」。この例は Heading 付き用紙なので、サインは Name の右に initial でする。followed by __0__ Pages of ～は、「この後に続くのはゼロ　ページのこと」だから、送信するのはこのページだけのことを意味している。Message pertaining to this transmission Message pertaining to this transmission の文はなくてもよい。Please contact the person named below if there is a problem with the transmission: Please contact the person named below if there is a problem with the transmission: と書いて、次に発信者の名前と連絡先を書くのが普通である。

[Sample letter 40]

The ABC Corporation
JFF 141 - UV Park - MC 1234
Los Angeles, CA 90089-1234
Phone No. (213) 777-2345
Fax No. (213) 777-2346

<u>FAX TRANSMISSION</u>

TO: <u>Heian University_____</u>
FAX NO: <u>234-781-0012_____</u>
ATTN: <u>Michio Otomo_____</u>
DATE: <u>8 October 20xx_____</u>
FROM: <u>Robert B. Stevenson_____</u>
PAGE ONE OF __1__ PAGES

MESSAGES

Mr. Otomo:

Thank you for your fax message of 5 October 20XX. On 4 October I had a long conversation with Mr. Matsushita. As I understand it, as the result of the illness of his parents, he and his wife are unable to travel to Japan at this time. That being the case, there would be nothing for me to do at Heian University. He and I agreed that it would not be good for me to go to Japan at this time. We thought it best to postpone the trip to a time more convenient for Mr. and Mrs. Matsushita.

I thank you for all the hard work you have already done on my behalf, and I truly apologize for any inconvenience this decision may cause you and other people who have gone to some trouble on my behalf.

I will reschedule the trip for some time that is mutually convenient to the Matsushitas and to me, and I will inform you of my new schedule at the earliest possible time. Please convey my apologies particularly to Mr. Wilkerson.

Thank you. Again, my most sincere apologies.

【注】署名はRobert B. Kaplanの右にするか, Thank you.の下方にする。PAGE ONE OF ___1___ PAGESとは送信枚数はこのページだけで1枚のこと。[例1]では 0 pages と書いてあった。That being the case,「こんな事情があるから」。on my behalf「私のために」。at the earliest possible time「出来る限り早く」

[Sample letter 41]

[Headingは省略]

Date: 15 April 20xx
To: Marilyn, Customer Service, ABC Publishing Co., Ltd.
FAX: 516-123-7777
From: Takeo Suzuki

In your 6 April 20xx e-mail, you asked for proof of payment of the *Journal of ABC Communication*.

Attached are the credit records which show that I paid for the Journal twice in 1998. Therefore please update your record.

I look forward to your reply. Thank you.

> 【注】サインは Heading のところに書いてある名前の右側に initial でするか，Thank you. の下に，左端から full name でする。credit records とは「支払った記録」のこと。

13.4　E-mailの英語

　今日のビジネス界を激変させたものに E-mail がある。E-mail はわれわれの生活やコミュニケーションの手段に革命を与えただけに，そこで使われる英語にミスがあるとビジネスに致命傷を与えることになる。

　E-mail は「電子メール」のことで，electronic mail の略である。今では，e-mail とハイフンを付けたり，email と付けない用法もあり，名詞，形容詞，動詞で使われる。

13.4.1　基本形式

発信者の氏名，住所，送信時刻などはウインドウの一番上にコンピューターが自動的に打ち出す。使用する機種やソフトにより多少異なるが，通常はその下に Subject (首題) および相手の名前と住所に当たるアドレス (Address) を打ち込む。Subject は，ここだけ読んで内容が理解出来るように，Topic と Purpose の両方を書くことを勧める。「1.10 Subject の書き方」(31 ページ) 参照。

ビジネスでは相手と始めて交信するとき以外は Dear Mr. Smith: のような堅苦しい Salutation は使わない。二回目からは Dear Tom, のようにファーストネームで始めるか，無視して，いきなり本文から始めてよい。個人的色彩が濃いメールでは Dear Mary, とか Hi Mary, とか Hello, Mary! などのようにファーストネームで始めることが多い。

本文は，時間を節約するため，インデントしない Full Block Style である。パラグラフとパラグラフの間は一行余分に空ける。

終わりは Sincerely, に当たるような格式ばった Complimentary Close (Closing) は用いない。ビジネスでは Salutation をタイプしたときは Best regards, の下にファーストネームをタイプして終えることが多い。Salutation をタイプしないときは名前だけをタイプして終える。個人的色彩が濃いメールでは送信者のファーストネームとアドレスだけをタイプして終わる場合が多い。中には, Bye, とか Bye for now, に続けてファーストネームで終える人もいる。

13.4.2　英語の特長

文字が画面に写しだされて読みにくいので Business letters よりも短文で，正確で，簡潔さが要求される。長い手紙は読み手の迷惑になるので避けたほうがよい。

電子メールなので，どのような記号になって相手に送信されて誤解を与えないとも限らない。大文字だけで書いてはならないし，長いダッシュ，アポストロフィ，引用符，アクセントの印，イタリックや下線などはできる限り使わないほうがよい。強調したければ，語・句や

文の前後を ＊ か < > で囲むとよい。

　特に注意すべき点に次の事項がある。
　① 文は短くする。
　② 公にできるものだけを送信する
　③ 必要なものだけを送信する
　④ 短い内容のものを送信する
　⑤ 要件は頭書に書く
　⑥ 書く会話，つまり口語表現が中心だから，人称代名詞の I; we; you などを多用する。

Thank you for your patience while waiting for my reply. I hope this information will be helpful.（私がご返事を差し上げるまでお待ちいただいたご辛抱にたいして厚くお御礼申し上げます[ご返事が遅れて申し訳ございません]。次の説明がお役に立つと思います）

I'm sorry for the delay in replying to your message. I had initiated a conversation with Dr. Smith last week, but due to travel, we have been unable to have any discussion about this.（[あなたのE-メールに]ご返事が遅れて申し訳ございません。先週スミス氏と話し合いを始めましたが，この件については氏が旅行中のため話し合うことが出来ないままになっております）

　のような書き出しか，いきなり

What is it that you would like me to consent?（私に何を同意して欲しいとおしゃるのですか）

のような単刀直入な文から始めてもよい。

　⑦ 特殊な略語を用いる。時間を短縮したいため次のような略語が多用される。しかし，受信者が理解できないような略語は使ってはならない。詳しくは，拙著『コンピューターとインターネットの英語の用語と文例』（日興企画）を参照。

13.4.3 多用される略語

AFAIK	as far as I know	(私が知っている限り)
BBL	be back later	(後で)
BTW	by the way	(ところで)
FWIW	for what it's worth	(価値があるかどうか分からないが；それはそれとして)
FYI	for your information	(ご参考までに)
IMHO	in my humble opinion	(私見では)
IMO	in my opinion	(私の意見では)
IOW	in other words	(言い換えれば)
LOL	laughing out loud	(大声で笑う)
OTOH	on the other hand	(他方)
TIA	Thanks in advance.	(まずはお願いまで)

⑧スマイリー記号を用いる

相手と会話をしている気分にいるため，感情を表すのにスマイリー(Smiley)[感情アイコン(Emoticon)]と呼ばれる記号を用いる。たとえば ;-) のような記号を右側を下にして縦にするとウインクをしている(Winking)ように見える。しかし小馬鹿にしたような印象を与えるので目上の人やビジネスでは避けた方がよい。参考までにいくつか紹介する。詳しくは，拙著『コンピューターとインターネットの英語の用語と文例』(日興企画)を参照。

13.4.4　スマイリー記号

:-)	Happy	(幸せ)
:-(	Sad	(悲しい)
:-&	Tongue-tied	（秘密）
:-||	Angry	（怒っている）
:-D	Laughing	（笑っている）
:-|	Grinning	（にたりとする）
%-)	Happy confused	(うれしくてちょっと当惑)
%-(	Sad confused	（悲しくて心を乱す）
:-/	Skeptical or perplexed	（当惑している）
:-\	Undecided	（未決定な）
:-P	Sticking tongue out	（正統であると主張する）
>:-<	Mean face	（不快な顔；送信者は怒っている）
>:->	Devilish remark	（極悪）
%-)	The sender is confused.	（送信者は困惑している）
:-x	The sender's lips are sealed.	（秘密です）

13.4.5 例文

[Sample 42]

Subject: Asking to Visit Your Hospital
Date: Mon, 15 June 20xx
From: Taro Suzuki tsuzuki@mn.abcd.ac.jp
To: Howard Ehlers hlers`apollogrp.edu

I study medicine at the ABC University in Japan. I would like to inspect the medical care system in the U.S. Is it possible for me to come and see your hospital some day between July 25 and August 10?

I look forward to your reply.

Taro Suzuki

【注】 用件だけを書いた簡単な E-mail の例。Subject は Re の例もある。

[Sample 43]

[Heading 省略]

Dear Subscription Department:

According to my credit card records, I paid a subscription fee twice (March and April) in 20xx for the JOURNAL OF ABC COMMUNICATION. Therefore please send the journals to me by the fee I paid.

I look forward to your reply.

> 【注】用件だけの簡単な例。E-mailでは余計なことを書かないほうがよい。

[Sample 44]

上のメールの返事

Thank you for your Jan. 20 e-mail concerning your subscription to the Journal of ABC Communication. According to our records, you are paid up to and through volume 27 (20xx) and would need to renew for volume 28 (20xx). If this has already been paid for, please send us proof of payment and I will update your record. Thank you.

Marilyn

> 【注】この返事は「ファクシミリの英語」の最後の [Sample letter 41] にあげた。update「最新のものに直す」

13.5 Short Business Reports

海外に支社や工場のある企業は手紙のほかに仕事上のレポートを交換することが多い。近ごろは，外国に工場を持つ日本企業が多いため，現地人と共同で作業をしたり，現地人と文書でもコミュニケートしなければねばならない。

これらの文書は Long Report と Short Report に分類される。Long Report は Formal Report ともいい，Short Report は Informal Report ともいう。企業では Short Report が多く，格式張ったレポート(Long Report; Formal Report)を書くことは稀であろう。

13.5.1 種類

Short Report は Memorandum ともいい，市況を報告するレポート（Market Reports），信用情報を中心としたレポート（Credit Information Reports），いろいろな情報を述べるレポート（Information Reports），経過や推移を述べるレポート(Progress Reports)，試験結果を述べるレポート(Examination Reports)，推薦するレポート(Recommendation Reports)などがある。これは種類で分類したものだが，記述式レポート(Descriptive Reports)，分析レポート(Analytic Reports)，評価するレポート(Evaluation Reports)などのように様式でも分類できる。

13.5.2 内容構成

Long Reports には，表紙(Cover)，扉(Title Page)，目次(Table of Contents)，アブストラクト(Abstract)，本文(Body Proper) [ここは序論(Introduction)，本論(Body)，結論(Conclusion)からなる]，付録(Supplementary Matter) [ここは，追加(Appendix)，参考文献(Bibliography)などからなる] で構成するのが普通である。

Short Report は，普通は Heading が付き，これと本文だけで構成さる。表紙，扉，目次，アブストラクトは付かない。忙しい人々が読むことが多いので冒頭文に全神経を傾注しなければならない。

Memorandum（社内連絡状）では Salutation も Closing も不要である。サインは発信者名をタイプしたところに Initial でする。

レポートの種類を問わず内容が異なっても，構成や展開法は類似している。ここでは，Short Report を中心として，その展開法を述べる。

13.5.3 Heading

Heading の部分は次の構成が普通である。

[例 1]

   To: John Smith, Manager
      Office of Ship Construction
      U.S. Department of Commerce
  From: Toshio Motohashi, Chief Engineer
      American Queen Lines
      Engineering Department
  Date: 10 March 20xx
 Subject: Policy Research on Population and Environment

通常の手紙と異なる点は，To:, From:, Date:, Subject: を必ず書くことである。また，Date の位置が From の下にくることが多いことと，Salutation と Complimentary Close を書かないことが多いことである。署名も From にタイプした名前の右端に initial ですることが多い。

同じ会社や社内では次の Heading が多用される。

[例 2]

MEMORANDUM

   TO: Dwight W. Zimmerman, Director of Marketing
   FROM: Mary Cornflower, Manager, Export Department
   DATE: September 5, 20xx
   SUBJECT: Proposed Central Filing System for Storage of
        Accounting Reports

13.5.4　Body of the Reports

Short Report は種類や長さに関係なく，目的 (Purpose)，調査結果 (Findings)，結論 (Conclusion)，推奨 (Recommendation) などを書くとよい。人称代名詞　I, we, you などの personal language を多用する。

日本では「冒頭で結論を述べよ」といわれているが，いきなり「.....の結果を得た」のように始めたのでは，読み手から Why? の質問がでる。そこで次のように書き出してから，それを説明する構成法が多い。

① 事実の証明から入る方法

「～は明白である」のような内容を表す。

Electronic industries' performance during the difficult 1965 to 1970 was evidence of the field's strength and stability. （1965年から1970年にわたる苦しい時代における電子産業の成果は，その分野の強さと安定性を証拠づけるものであった）

② 目的を述べる方法

目的を明示しないと，読み手には書き手の真意が理解できないので目的は必ず述べること。欧米では，「目的を書かない人は文章を書く資格がない」と言われているほどである。目的には二つあり，一つは What you have done. [What you will do.] (何をした[する]) かであり，もう一つは What will you be done? (何をして欲しいか)である。前者は Technical Purpose (技術上の目的)とか Investigation (調査)といわれ，後者は Communication Purpose (伝達上の目的)といわれている。

The purpose of this report is to examine the feasibility of stretching glass. (本レポートの目的は，ガラスを延ばすことができることを調査したものです) [Technical Purposeの例]。読み手が「何故か」の質問を出す懸念があれば，その背景か①を説明する必要がある。

The purpose of this report is to explain to you the scope and structure of the proposed training and to request approval for such a training session. (本レポートの目的は，提案した訓練の範囲と構成を説明し，その訓練の開催の承認を得ることです)

③ 問題提起法

読み手の注意を引く書き方だが，いや味にならないように書くこと。

The radiator hose clamp has often failed on our cars produced during the period between March 1 - 31, 1999. (1999年の3月1日～31日に生産されえた当社の自動車では，ラジエーター・ホースの締金がよく故障しています)

④ 問題点から入る方法

現在，「このような問題がある」から始める方法

The present hoist system is inadequate to lift ABC models from the tank for temporary storage. (現在の巻上げ方式は，一時的に保管するタンクから，ABCモデルを持ち上げるのに不適切です)

⑤ 「～は非常な好評を博している」のような内容を述べる方法

The ABC microwave oven continues to enjoy tremendous retail success and consumer acceptance. (ABC社の電子レンジは，小売りで素晴らしい成功をしており，消費者からの受けもよい)

⑥ 歴史的背景から入る方法

すでに起こった事実を述べて読み手の心をとらえる方法

On July 1, 20xx, ABC Airlines authorized specification changes on the airship. (20xx年7月1日に，ABC航空会社は，飛行船の仕様変更を正式に許可した)

次に Negative Example と Revised Example を紹介する。前者はアメリカの大学生が書いた Short Report である。両者の論理構成の相違に注意すること。

13.5.5 例文

[Sample 45]

[Negative Example]
[Heading 部は省略]
SUBJECT: New Filing System for Storage of ATPs and Test Reports

The System Analysis Department has the responsibility of reviewing the Final Acceptance Test Procedures (ATPs) for the components of the new satellite communications system. The Final ATPs are compared with the original (ATPs) and the subsequent Test Reports to check that all Government comments and red-line changes have been incorporated. Deadlines, set by the production department, have to be met in reviewing the Final ATPs. However, it is often a time consuming task to find all the original ATPs and the Test Reports because they are scattered in various offices about the department, thus making it hard to meet the deadlines.

This observation led to my search for a more efficient method of reviewing the Final ATPs that would:
1) allow a person to find the reports without having to search from one person's office to another, and
2) allow any person to find the necessary reports.

The purpose of this report is to recommend for implementation, an efficient system of finding the original ATPs and Test Reports so that all production deadlines can be met.

In my analysis of different systems of retrieval of the original ATPs and the Test Reports, a filing system appeared to be the most effi-

cient. Therefore, I recommend that a filing system, alphabetized by component name, be implemented as soon as possible. This method would have the advantage of:
1) being compact so it could be centrally located, thus eliminating the problems of searching for the various reports, and
2) having an alphabetical index in the beginning so that anyone could retrieve the information contained in the file.

With this filing system implemented, the Final ATPs could be processed more efficiently, enabling production deadlines to be met.

[Revised]
    SUBJECT: Proposed Central Filing System for Storage of ATPs and Tests Reports

The Systems Analysis Department is responsible for reviewing the final Acceptance Test Procedures (APTs) for the components of the new satellite communications system. The final ATPs are compared with the original ATPs and the subsequent Test Reports to check that all government recommendations and changes have been incorporated. Deadlines set by the Production Department must be met in reviewing the final ATPs. However, it is often a time-consuming task to find all the original ATPs and Test Reports because they are scattered in various offices.

This observation let to a search for a more efficient method of reviewing the final ATPs. The method would allow anyone to find the reports without searching from one office to another. This report recommends a method for implementation

Analysis of different retrieval systems showed a manual filing system to be the most cost-effective. Therefore, I recommend that a filing system, alphabetized by component name, be implemented as soon as possible. This filing system would have the advantage of being compact so it could be centrally located. An alphabetical index at the front of the file would make it possible to retrieve ATPs and Test Reports quickly.

> 【注】is responsible for ～「～に責任を持つ」。reviewing「を再調査する」。Acceptance Test Procedures (APTs)と括弧内にAPTsとしたことは，今後は略語のAPTsを用いることを意味する。have been incorporated「組み入れられている」。a time-consuming task「時間を無駄にする仕事」。they are scattered in various offices「それらは一箇所にまとまらないで社内のいろいろな所に散らばっている」。This observation let to a search for ～「この観察により～の調査をすることにした」。implementation「実行」。different retrieval systems「いろいろな情報検索方式」。a manual filing system「手による書類整理方式」。the most cost-effective「最も経済的な；最も効果的な」。component name「構成要素の名前」。have the advantage of being compact「場所を取らないという利点がある」。retrieve「情報を検索する[引き出す]」。

13.6 議事録

　グローバル化した現在，外資系企業のみならず国外に支社や工場を持つ企業は少なくとも一週間に一度はミーティングを開く。その際，ミーティングの内容を記録に残し，後々の参考にするためファイルする慣わしがある。この会議を記録した書類，つまり「議事録」を英語で minutes という。ミーティングで承認された事項は公認されたことを意味するため，法手続きの証拠としても利用される。したがって，意図的に内容を変更してはならず，公平，明確，正確，簡潔であらねばならない。

13.6.1 記載事項

会社により記載事項や形式は異なるが，基本的な事柄は同じである。

1. Name of Organization（企業名）
2. Place, Date, Time of Meeting（会議の場所、日時、時間）
3. Kind of Meeting（会議の種類）[Weekly Meeting; Monthly Meeting; Special Meetingなど]
4. Name of the Presiding Person（議長名）
5. List of Those Present and Absent（出席者・欠席者名）
6. Reference of the Minutes of the Previous Meeting（前回の議事録の参考事項）
7. Account of All Reports, Motions, Resolutions（すべての報告、動議、決議の詳細な記事）
8. Date, Time, and Place of the Next Meeting（次の会合の日時と場所）
9. Time of Adjournment（終了時間）

13.6.2 記録者の注意点

1. すべてを記録しないで，要点だけを書く
2. 討議内容は書かないで，決定事項だけを箇条書きにする
3. 賛成・反対に記録者は自分の見解とか意見を書いてはならない

   [例] As usual, Mr. Smith disagreed with the committee.
   （何時ものようにSmith氏はその委員に賛成しなかった）

   excellent, fair, good, irrelevant（的外れの），poorのような感情を表す単語も避けたほうがよい。

   記録係はテープレコーダーを使うとよいが，使用するときは，出席者に予めその旨を伝えておくべきである。

13.6.3 会議についての諸注意

1. 話をするときは，まず要点を明確，簡潔に述べる
2. 会議に出席する前にデータを集め，そのデータを論理的に述べる準備をしておく

3. 仕事以外の話題は避ける
4. 反対意見をいうときは，you という個人を指す代名詞は避けて，事実や結果に対して反対する
5. 会議が終了したら速やかに退場する

13.6.4 議題，協議事項，議事の書き方

まず，ミーティングの前に配布する議題，協議事項の書き方から始めよう。

[例1]

Software Improvements Committee
Agenda for July 25, 20xx
(20xx年7月25日開催の議題)

[例2]

Software Improvements Committee
Agenda of Faculty Meeting
July 25, 20xx

この次に議題と議長名と肩書きをタイプする。

[例3]

  1. Recent Divisional Reorganization
  2. Software Marketing
  3. Filing Problems

William Bailey
Chairperson

議事録の形式は企業や機関により異なるが，内容は基本的には同じである。

13.6.5　構成要素と実例

① 企業[機関]名 (Name of Organization)を書く

通常は用紙の上端の真中に書く。

[例]

    Minutes of Meeting of the Software Improvements Committee
                      The Reverton Corporation
                          September 15, 20xx

常任委員会(Standing Committee), 特別委員会 (Ad hoc Committee), 定例会議 (Regular Meeting); 月例会議 (Monthly Meeting), 一週一度の会議(Weekly Meeting)のなどがある。種類によりMinutes of Meeting of ~とか, Minutes of Standing Committee of ~とかMinutes of Regular Meeting of ~のように書く。

社内だけに配布する議事録であれば社名は書かなくてよい。

② 場所と時間 (Place and Time)を書く

ここに開催日を書いてもよい。

[例1]

        Place and Time: Tenth-floor Conference Room
                    Wednesday July 25, 20xx 10 A.M.

この部分を次のように文章にしてもよい。

[例2]

        Time and Place: The meeting was held on Wednesday, July 25, 20xx, in the Tenth-floor Conference Room.

        The chairperson, William Bailey, called the meeting to order at 10.00 A.M.

[例 3]

    Time and Place: The meeting was called to order by Chairperson William Bailey at 10 A.M., July 25, 20xx in the Tenth-floor Conference Room.

③ 議長名 (Presiding) を書く

通常は書類のHeadingの下方に書くが，Time and Placeで書けば，ここに書く必要はない。

[例]　Presiding:　William Bailey

④ 出席者名 (Attendance) を書く

英語はAttendanceでもPresentでもよい。肩書きの上位から順に書くか，Family Nameをアルファベット順に書く。肩書き，敬称などは付けない。

[例]

    Present: G. Smith, E. Gerald, Y. Nagata, G. Ryan, J. Rose, L. Cote, T. Suzuki, B. Morton, Y. Watanabe, K. Caldwell, W. Hiller, T. Kiley (Secretary),

    Absent: R. Baker, C. Emerson

議事をとる人は名前の次に (Secretary) と書くか (minutes) と書くのが普通である。

⑤ 前の会議の議事録の修正などの有無 (Reference to the minutes of the previous meeting) に触れる。もし修正があれば，読み上げて承認 (accept) を得る。次のように記録する。

[例 1]

    The minutes of the August 30 meeting were read by Smith and approved.

[例 2]
  The minutes of the August 30, 20xx meeting was read.
  The following correction was made.
修正がなければ，触れなくてもよいし，次のように書いてもよい。
  Old Business: None.

⑥ 討議・審議・決定事項 (Account of all reports, motions, or resolutions made) を書く

ここが，議事録の本文である。Discussions とか New Business の項目を立ててよい。次の点に注意。

* 私情を入れないで，明確・正確・簡潔に議事を採る。
* 人名には肩書きや敬称は付けない。

Manager of Export Department, Mr. Thomas Carter と書かないで，T. Carter でよい。もし Mr. Carter と書いたら，他に人も同じに敬称を付ける。

* Agenda の順に書く。詳細は時間順に書く。
* 投票があれば，投票数 (Number of votes) と賛否 (For and Against) の数を書く。
* 動議 (Motions) は一語一語発言された通りに発言者を明記して筆記しなければならない。動議以外は要約して書き，討議事項はパラフレーズしてよい。
* 議論された項目ごとに Topic:, Discussion:, Action Taken: のような見出しを立てて書いていくと整理しやすい。
* bad, good, very, extremely のような曖昧な修飾語（句）は使わない。bad report ではなく *inaccurate* report（不正確なレポート）とか *misleading* report（誤りのあるレポート）が明確でよい。

[例]
Discussions: The minutes of the August 10 meeting were approved in the form distributed to members.（8月10日に開催された会議の議事録は委員に配布された形式で承認された）

Smith explained the recent reorganization of ~. Gerald explained the key issue of ~. The request by Nagata for ~ was discussed. Ryan made a motion that the system be granted ~. Cote seconded the motion, which passed unanimously.（スミスが～に～についての最近の再改革について説明し，ジェラルドが～についての重要な問題を説明をした。永田が要請した議題が論議された。ライアンがそのシステム認めるべきだと提議し，コートが支持し，満場一致で可決された）

Morton presented a written financial report, which was approved on motion by Coldwell and was seconded by Suzuki (copy attached).（モートンが財務報告書を提出し，コールドウェルが動議を承認し，鈴木が支持した[コピー添付]）

Hiller recommended that air conditioning in the lab, which costs $5,000 per month, be eliminated. There was various objections to his recommendation, and it was agreed that this topic would be discussed further before final action is taken.（研究所の空調は毎月5,000ドルもかかるので取り外すべきであるとヒラーが提案したが，種々の理由で反対があり，今後さらに議論をしてから決めることで合意した）

Gerald presented a report on the May activities of HVAC Department.（ジェラルドがHVAC部の5月の活動に関する報告書を提出した）

In paragraph 5 of point 2, "5000 miles" was replaced with "500" miles. The minutes were then unanimously approved.（問題点2段落5で，5000マイルが500マイルに変えられた。次いでこの議事録は満場一致で承認

された)

Chairperson Smith began the meeting by describing the financial report on the project. (スミス議長は，そのプロジェクのついての財務報告書を説明して会を始めた)

Morton offered two alternatives:
1. Improvement: Improvement will be made to the existing profile.
2. Improvement extended: Same as alternative 1, but add ABC improvement ...

Chairperson Smith then asked for comments on the alternatives. Hiller asked whether Cote had considered if any of the alternatives would be affected by .... Cote responded that he did not know....

Chairperson Smith indicated that he would recommend to the president that ....

There being no more suggestions on ..., Chairperson Smith asked for a vote on the three alternatives. They were approved as a package unanimously.

After considerable discussion, the motion to add a new budget in the International Sales Department was defeated by a vote of 7 to 5.

(モートンが二つの代案を提議した：
改善1　現在のプロフィールへの改善
改善2 [拡張した]　1と同じだが，ABCの改善が加えられた。

次いでスミス議長が代案についてのコメントを要請した。代案の何れかが　〜　によって影響を受けるかどうかをコートが考えたことがあるかヒラーが尋ねた。コートは知らないと応答した。

スミス議長は ～ (that 以下のこと)を社長に推奨すると明示した。

～ に関して提案がなかったので，スミス議長は3つの案について投票を求めた。一括提案として満場一致で承認された。

かなりの議論の後で，国際営業部に新しい予算を追加する動議は投票の結果5対7で認められなかった)

以上のほかに，次のような動詞も頻繁に用いられる。

  Gerald *suggested* that .... He *proposed* that ....
  Ryan *recommended* that .... He *pointed out* that ....

⑦ 次の会議の予定日時を書く

次の会議の日程が決まっていれば明記するのが普通である。

[例1]

Next Meeting: The next meeting will be held on Thursday, August 25, at 10 A.M, in the Board Room. (次の会議は会議室で8月25日，木曜日，午前10時の予定)

[例2]

Finally, chairperson Smith called for a special meeting of the committee on August 25 at 10 A.M. to finalize the strategy for the approval.(最後に，スミス議長は，承認を求める戦術を最終的にまとめるために，臨時の会議を8月25日，午前10時に開くことを要請した)

⑧ 新規事項

新しい討議事項があるか，ないかを書く。

[例]

New business

Chairperson Smith asked if there was any new business. There was none. (新規事項：スミス議長は新しい議題があるかを尋ねたが，なかった)

⑨ 終わりの時間を書く
[例1]

Adjournment: The meeting was adjourned at 11:45 A.M.（終了：11時45分終了）

[例2]

Chairperson Smith adjourned the meeting at 5:00.

Adjournment と Next Meeting を一緒にして，次のように書いてもよい。

[例3]

There being no further business, the meeting was adjourned at 10:55 a.m. The next regular meeting is scheduled for Thursday, August 25, at 10:00 a.m.（これ以上の議題がなかったため，10時55分散会。次の定例会議は8月15日，木曜日，午前10時の予定）

⑩ 結びの文

最後は，次のように書いて終える。

[例]

Respectfully submitted,

   (Signature) (Signature)
   Tenar Kiley John Smith
   Secretary   Chairperson

しかし，Respectfully submitted, は今でも実際に見られるが時代遅れとも言われている。

⑪ 資料の配布者を書く

次に配布先を次のようにタイプする。

[例1]

  Distribution:
  Committee Members: G. Smith, E. Gerald, Y. Nagata, G.

Ryan, J. Roes, L. Cote, T. Suzuki, B. Morton, Y. Watanabe, K. Caldwell, W. Hiller, R. Baker, C. Emerson

Others: Mr. Newell, Mrs. Spitzer, Mr. Yabe

２ページ目からは用紙の上部に次のようにタイプする。
[例2]
Minutes of the August 25 Meeting　　　　　Page 2

13.7　English in Negotiation

　話し合い (negotiation) や発表 (presentation) は，われわれに四六時中付きまとう。こちらの意見と相手の意見が異なるとき negotiation に入ることが多い。また，新製品ができたり，新しいアイデアが生まれると，それを効果的に説明しなければならない。自分も相手も満足するように話を進めるにはコミュニケーション技術が必要になる。コミュニケーションを上手にしなければ negotiation や presentation で成果は期待できないので，ここではコミュニケーションを成功させるときに頻出する英語の例をビジネスの場を中心に紹介する。

　negotiation や presentation で，まず心掛けることは，相手から信頼され，尊敬されるように努めることであり，無用な障害 (roadblock) をなくすように努めることである。また，人間関係を大切にするよう心がけ，相手を批判したり，相手にマイナスのイメイジを与えるような言葉を使うことも避けたほうがよい。絶対に相手を非難 (criticize) してはならない。negotiation と presentation をする際に注意すべき事柄を述べる。

13.7.1　相手を非難する英語

相手を非難して感情に走る次のような表現は，余程のことがない限り使用しないほうがよい。使用を余儀なくされた場合には抑揚には注意

が肝要である。感情に走って強い抑揚で言わないほうがよい。
* "You ought to say you are sorry." は避ける方がよい。相手をけなす (moralizing) ことになる。
* "Say 'Yes.'" とか "Do it now." とか "Do it or else ...!" は避ける方がよい。命令して相手を脅す (threatening) ことになる。
* "What a dope!" は「この間抜けめ」のような意味になるので，相手の名前を言いながらだと暴言になる。
* "You are irritating me." は避ける方がよい。問題の原因を究明しながらこのような英語を言う人がいるが，相手を信用しないことになるので避けるほうがよい。
* "Why didn't you ...?" は避ける方がよい。不信感を抱くことになる。
* "I think you are smarter than he." は「あなたは彼よりも頭がよいですね」のことだが，気のない賞賛 (faint praise) になるので言わないほうがよい。
* "Who did it?" のような個人を追求しない。誤りなどを見つけたら "What happened?" がよい。

感情に脅かされるような状態になったら，発言しないで，「10まで数えてから口を開くことを勧める」(I recommend you count to 10 before you speak.) か，「暫くの間その場を離れて冷静になってからその問題について話し合うことを勧める」(I recommend you walk away for a moment to cool down before discussing the issues.) が定説になっている。

13.7.2 心に留めておくべき点

話し合いを成功させようと思ったら，次の事柄を念頭に置くことを勧める。

1. 主観的でなく客観的に述べること
2. 人を責めないで事柄をせめること
3. 否定的な環境を作らないで肯定的な環境を作ること
4. 問題・解決（problem/solution）の方法を忘れないこと
5. お互いの関係を良くしようと心がけること

6. 自分と異なる意見でも注意深く耳を傾け，話を逸らせないで適切に対応すること
7. 自分ばかり発言しないで，相手にも発言の時間を与えること
8. 本来の議題から逸脱しないように注意すること
9. 習慣の違いに注意すること
10. 意見は明確に，論理的に述べること

13.7.3　避けるべき態度

だれでも会議は円滑に進み，早く，自分の期待していた通りに終えようと思うであろう。そのためには，少なくとも次の事項を心がけるとよい。

1. 失敗をあれこれ理由をつけて言い訳しない
2. 会議の邪魔をしない
3. 相手を攻撃して，自分の優位性を高めない
4. すべての意見に反対して，相手を不愉快にさせない
5. 自分の意見に固執して，相手の意見を聞かない
6. 相手を指でささない
7. 必要以上に大声を挙げない
8. 途中で席を外さない

13.7.4　避けるべき英語

negotiation を成功させようと思ったら，相手に不快感を与える次のような単語は避けなければならない。

1. You は「言う」な

日本語の「あなた」に当たる英語は you だが、日本語と違って，英語の you には失礼になることがあるので，相手にとってプラスになる事柄のとき以外はその使用を避けた方がよい。

* 「あなた間違えましたよ」と優しくいったつもりで "You made a mistake." というと相手を攻撃したことになる。一緒に働いてい

るのであれば，"We might make a mistake."がよい。思いやりのwe とでも覚えておくとよいだろう。
* 「なぜあなたは私に怒鳴るのですか」のような日本語を "Why do you yell at me?" と言うのではなく，"I prefer we have a calm down." と you ではなく we を用いることでソフトになる。
* "You are not very helpful."（あなたはあまり助けにならない）のように，You を主語にするのは失礼で相手を責めることになるから，You を主語にしないで，"It is not very helpful." のように It を主語にして表現するとソフトになる。
* "You make me so mad!"（あなたには頭に来る）ではなく "I felt angry." がよいが，これも相手から目をそらせて言うべきである。
* "If you don't do this, I will never work with you again."（このことをしてくれないなら，二度と一緒に仕事をいたしません）よりは，"When we both do this, we'll work better as a team, produce better results."（二人でこの仕事をすれば，チームとして良い結果が得られるし，よい結果が出るでしょう）が相手に与える印象がよい。

2. 相槌のつもりで yes を使わない

相手の話に耳を傾けながら，「はい」「はい」「うん」「うん」と相手に相槌を打っているときに "Yes. Yes." というと，相手は賛成してくれたと思ってどんどん話を先へ進めてしまう。賛成していないなら "Yes." とか "OK." と言わないほうがよい。相槌を打つつもりで，"Yes. Yes." と言っていて，だいぶ相手の話が進んでから，But, ... と切り返す日本人がいるが、相手は，今まで賛成していながら，なぜ急に反対するのだろうかと戸惑う。耳を傾けるだけのときは "Mm, Mm." がよい。賛成ならば "I agree." と言い，反対ならば，その理由を上手に説明するとよい。

同様に，誤解を与える単語に "Maybe." がある。"Yes." と同じぐらい "Maybe." を連発する日本人が多いようだ。日本人の使う "Maybe." は "No." に近い意味のようだが，米・英では，話し手は50％ぐらいの

可能性を意識して答えているのである。

3. Listen to me. は失礼

「ちょっと聞いてください」と軽い気持ちで "Listen to me." と言うと，相手に何かを強要することになり失礼になることがあるので注意をした方がよい。相手にプラスの要因を与える事柄以外は命令文で言うのは避けたほうが無難である。相手に，不快感をできるだけ与えないで依頼するには語調が大切な要素を占めるので，1.1「大切な語調」，1.2「Softenerが大切」を参照。

4. I can't understand you. は失礼

「あなたのことが理解できないのです」のようなことは言わないほうがよい。特に，can't は強く否定することになるので失礼になる。「私があなたのことが理解できなくて申し訳ありません」の気持ちで "I'm sorry." でよい。"I'm sorry." は，相手の言ったことが分からなくて「申し訳ありませんが，もう一度言っていただけますか」のようなときにも使われる。

5. No.を避ける

相手の要求にたいして "No." と言ったのではすべてがお終いである。できる限り肯定で打ち消すように心がけることを勧める。詳しくは，1.4「打消しよりも肯定で」，拙著『英語感覚が身につく本』(南雲堂)，『使える英語が見えてくる』(洋販出版)，『英語の落とし穴』(大修館書店) 参照。

6. 受動態を避ける

"Your idea is understood."（あなたの考えは理解されました）では誰が理解したのかが分からないので，"I understand you idea." と能動態で表現すると，「理解した人」が明確になる。

"Your products will be bought."（貴社の品物は買われるでしょう）も

誰が買うか定かでないので，"Many people will buy your products." (多くの人が貴社の品物を買うでしょう) としたほうがよい。詳しくは，1.5「受動態と能動態を使い分ける」を参照。その他については，1.1「大切な語調」，1.2「Softener が大切」を参照。

13.7.5　好感[悪印象]を与える単語

ビジネスの世界では相手にお世辞をいったり，へつらったり，機嫌をとる必要はないが，好印象を与える単語と悪印象を与える単語があることを忘れたはならない。

好印象を与える単語として appreciate, beautiful, freedom, kindness, obstacles, persevering, pretty, slender, successful, trust などがある。

悪印象を与えるるとして，cheap, delinquent, demand, fat, fraud, negligent obstinate, scrawny などがある。

とにかく，プラスかマイナスかのイメージを与える単語があるので，分からなければ辞書で確認することを勧める。少しでもマイナスの意味合いがある単語は使わないほうがよい。英英辞典で Taboo，英和辞典で卑語と明示してある単語は使うべきではない。

尋ねるときは，"What do you think ...?", "Tell me about ...," "Why weren't you satisfied with ...?", "Would you agree that ...?" などの形式の質問や依頼は相手に話をさせる機会を与えるため，相手の考えが分かるので使用するとよい。

13.7.6　同意を求める表現

1. Tag question（平叙文の後に簡単な疑問文）を用いる。
   "That's a good idea, *isn't it*?"
2. 同意を求める疑問文を添える。
   "That's a fascinating plan, *don't you think*?"
   "We'd better finish this today, *don't you agree*?"
3. "(Do you) agree ..." で始める。
   "*Don't you agree* that his idea is too risky?"　risky「危険」

"*Are you in agreement* with us?"
"*Do you agree* to help us if we need help?"

13.7.7　同意する表現
"I agree."
"I know what you mean."
"I think so, too."
"Certainly."
"O.K. with me."
"Fine with me."
"That's for sure."
"It's a deal."
"I'll go along with that."
"I'm completely satisfied with everything."
"It was satisfactory."
"Everything is fine, thank you."
"Everything is just perfect."
"I'm happy enough with it."
"Good enough."
"No bad."
"It is O.K."

13.7.8　反対意見の表現
柔らかい口調で言うことを勧める。
"I don't think so."
"I'm not so sure."
"I don't agree."
"I find I can't agree with you."
"I can't go along with you on that."
"I refuse."

"No deal."
"No way."
"I have a complaint."
"I'm a bit disappointed with the plan."
"I'm little dissatisfied with the program."
"I feel bad that I can't help you more."

13.7.9　相手が憤慨しているか否かを聞く表現

"Did I insult you?"
"Are you angry about something?"
"Are you angry with me?"
"What are you so angry about?"
"What happened?"
"What's the matter?"

13.7.10　怒りを抑えるように依頼する表現

"Maybe you're a little too sensitive."
"Please calm down."
"Take it easy."
"Please don't be so touchy."
"Let's try to hold our temper."
"Getting angry won't help."
"Don't get hot under the collar."

13.7.11　注意すべき表現

Worse: You are expected to be here on time. (あなたは時間どおりにくると思われていましたよ) [批判しないほうがよい]。

Better: You said that you would be here at ten o'clock.. (あなたは10時にお出でなるとおしゃいましたね)

Worse: You are always late for work every day.（あなたは何時も，毎日，仕事に遅れるね）[相手を非難しないほうがよいし，alwaysは誇張である]
Better: What is the reason for being late? (なぜ遅れたのですか)

Worse: Spare me your excuses. (言い訳は聞きたくありません)
　　　　[批判しないほうがよい]
Better: What happened to make you do that? (何が原因であなたにそんなことをさせたのでしょう)

Worse: How often were you late this week? (今週は何度遅れたの)
　　　　[明確に言うほうがよい]
Better: You are late twice. (あなたは今週二度遅れましたね)

Worse: You did a fine job.(素晴らしい仕事をしましたね)
　　　　またはIt was better than usual.（何時もよりよいですよ）
　　　　(明確に言ったようがよい)
Better: You finished an hour's job in half the time. (あなたは一時間の仕事を30分で終えましたね)

Worse: Excellent! Way to go! (素晴らしね。郡を抜いていますよ)
　　　　[良い仕事をしてどうなのかがわからない]
Better: Thanks for giving it you all. (全力を尽くしていただき有難う)

Worse: I don't understand what you said. (あなたの仰ったことは理解できません) [あまりにもきつい表現である]
Better: Before you continue, please sum up the points you've made.（次の項目に入る前に，これまでのことを要約していただけませんか）

Worse: To speak clearly you must open your mouth wide and speak in a louder voice. (はっきりお話をしたければ，もっと口を開けて，大声で話しなさい)[相手を責めてはならない。Say it once more. [または Say it again. も「もう一度言え」くらい失礼な表現だから避けたほうがよい]

Better: Sorry, I didn't hear you.(申し訳ありません。聞こえませんでした)

Avoid: You're going to get in trouble if you don't get rid of that attitude. (態度お変えにならないと，トラブルに巻き込まれることになるでしょう) [曖昧にしないで，起こりそうなことを明確に伝えるほうがよい]

Avoid: This is not my job —it's his. (それは私の仕事ではありません。彼の仕事です) [目上の人へは避けるべき表現である。目的を明確に言い，自分の責任を明示することが肝要である)。

Avoid: You take care of your work and I'll take care of mine. (あなたはあなたの仕事を，私は私の仕事しましょう) [ビジネスではあくまでも協力することが大切である]

Avoid: This is what you ought to do. (これはあなたの仕事です) [How about trying (doing) this?] は好ましい表現。

13.7.12 適切な反応表現

1. 不合理と思える質問をされたときの答え方

    Please give me some more details so that I can understand the reason for your request. (あなたのご要求に対する理由を理解したいのでもっと詳細にお伝えください)

2. 個人攻撃をされたときの答え方

    Let's concentrate on the issues and avoid personalities. (その問題に集中し，個人のことは避けましょう)

3. 相手が抗議をして立ち去ろうするときの押さえる言い方

I have something to discuss with you, so please stay after the others leave. (あなたと私は大切な話し合いが残っておりますので、他の人が帰ってもあなたにはここに留まって貰いたいのです)

4. 怒鳴られたときの言い方

Please calm down and speak slowly and clearly so that I can understand you. I'm very interested in hearing what you have to say. (あなたの仰りたいことを伺いたいので、もう少し穏やかに、ゆっくり、明確に、お話いただきたいのですが)

13.8 English in Presentation

13.8.1 挨拶 (Greeting)

挨拶から始めるのが普通である。英語はほとんど決まっている。

[例] Thank you very much for coming to this meeting. First of all, I want to thank you all for coming today. (本日は、お忙しいところ、この会にご出席いただき有難うございました。まず、お集まりいただきましいた皆さまに御礼申し上げます)

13.8.2 製品・アイデアの説明 (Explanation of a New Product or New Idea)

挨拶と出席してくれたお礼がすむと、製品か新しいアイデアの説明に入るのが普通である。

[例] Now I'd like to show you our new state-of-the-art printer. I'm confident that you will benefit from this product. (では、当社の新型で、現代の技術を取り入れたプリンターをご紹介いたします。この製品は貴社に貢献するものと確信いたします。

13.8.3 特長の説明 (Explanation of Advantages)

ここで、製品などの特長を説明するか、パンフレットなどがあれば、それに触れる。

[例1] Now, for a second, look at the handout?（ここで，お手元の資料をちょっとご覧下さい）

[例2] Now, will you open the pamphlet at page 5.（さあ，パンフレットの5ページをお開きください）

[例3] We have developed this printer with the idea of a sharp image.（当社では，鮮明な画像を主眼にしてこのプリンターを開発しました）

[例4] We have developed this product with a greater recycling ratio in mind.（当社では，リサイクルの歩留まりを念頭にしてこの製品を開発いたしました）

[例5] I'll make a little presentation to you about some features of this printer.（皆さんに，このプリンターの特長を少しご説明いたしましょう）

[例6] We have so many models, so we can satisfy different consumers' needs.（たくさんのモデルを用意しておりますので，いろいろな消費者のご要望を満足させることができます）

[例7] The new design is another advantage of this printer.（デザインの斬新さもこのプリンターのもう一つの有利な点です）

[例8] I'll show you some slides.（スライドをお見せしましょう）

13.8.4　説明の終了 (Closing the Explanation)

特長や納期などを説明し，presentation を終えるときの言い方は殆ど決まっている。

[例] Thank you very much for your time. We're getting near the end. I'll be glad to answer any questions now.（お時間をいただき有難うございました。終わりの時間が近づいて参りました。ご質問をお受けいたします）

13.8.5　質問に答える (Answering Questions)

[例1] If you have any questions, please don't hesitate to ask.（ご質

問がございましたら，ご遠慮なくどうぞ）

[例2] A：Can this product compete in the American markets?

B：Yes, I can guarantee that.

（A：この製品はアメリカの市場で他の製品と対抗できますか。

B：はい，保証いたします）

【注】I can guarantee that. は，アメリカでは You bet! とか You bet it can. などともいう。

[例3] A：Why are you so confident about the quality?

B：The product passed every test we ran.

（A：なぜそんなに品質に自信がおありですか。B：あらゆる限りのテストを受けた製品なのです）

[例4] We have repeatedly and strictly carried out performance tests.

（性能テストを繰り返し，厳格に行ってまいりました）

[例5] I'll be glad to go over it one more time.

（もう一度ご説明いたします）

【注】聴衆から I couldn't follow some of the new technology.（ご説明の新技術の辺が理解できませんでした）のような質問が出たときに利用できる）

13.8.6　終了 (Closing the Presentation)

終わりには，相手の印象に残るように，製品のPRか取引の申し出を簡単にすると効果があがる。

[例1] I am sure that our printer will make you a lot of money.（当社のプリンターが貴社の利益につながることと確信いたします）

[例2] We are eager to export our advanced printer to your market.（当社は貴市場へ当社の一歩先んじたプリンターを輸出することを心から望んでおります）

[例3] We must ask that all of this information is strictly confidential.（この内容はすべて極秘にお願いします）

[例4] We hope we will be able to establish a mutually profitable business relationship.（貴社と当社の双方が利益になるような取引

関係の成立を心から希望しております)

[例5] It's time to start wrapping things up.　Thank you very much.
（時間が参りましたので終わらせていただきます。有難うございました）

13.9　人物紹介状と推薦状

推薦状を依頼されたら，先方が人物紹介状 (Letter of Reference) か推薦状 (Letter of Recommendation) かのどちらを要求しているかを確かめる必要がある。両者は内容が異なるからである。宛先の名前が分からないときの Salutation は従来は To Whom It May Concern: とされていたが，時代遅れと冷たい印象を受信人に与えるので，現在では Dear Director: や Dear Admission Officer: や Dear Dean: や Dear Graduate Chair: のように責任者の肩書きを書くのがよいといわれている。

13.9.1　人物紹介状

通常，短くて簡単である。形式は決まっていないが，紹介する人物の名前を書き，経歴，人物についての長所を簡単に書き，「以上推薦する」で終わるのが普通である。

13.9.1.1　書出しの例

Mr. Taro Suzuki 〜. のように，いきなり推薦される人の名前から書き始めることもあるが，I am happy to 〜. とか It is a pleasure to〜. のように softener を使って，決まった書き出しをするのが普通である。
[例]
　　Dear Mr. Coldwell:

　　I am happy to provide the information you requested regarding Taro Suzuki, with the understanding that this information will be kept confidential.

で始めたり，

Dear Mr. Fisher:
Taro Suzuki worked as an salesperson at the ABC Company Ltd. last winter and I am happy to comment on his experience here as you asked.

で始め，次に，

Mr. Suzuki proved to be a quick learner and trustworthy employee.

とか，

Everyone agrees that he is intelligent, dependable, and well organized. I would highly recommend Taro Suzuki for the position of consultant.

ぐらいで終えてよい。

13.9.1.2　例文
次に Letter of Reference の例を示す。

[Sample letter 46]

Dear Program Director:

Mr. Smith has been teaching composition in our department, the English and American Literature Department, since April 1980 and has been doing an excellent job. He has been a conscientious teacher and has a fine attendance record.

He has a good relationship with his students, gets along well with his fellow teachers, and has contributed greatly to our composition program at ABC University.

Sincerely yours,

> 【注】同僚か役職に就いている先生にお願いした、ごく簡単な推薦状の例。まず、何を何時から教えている（いた）かを書く。その勤務状態や性格などはどうであったかも、誉めることは分かっていても書く必要がある。conscientious「真面目な；良心的な」。gets along well〜「〜と仲良くやって行く；うまくやって行く」。fellow「同僚の」。

[Sample letter 47]

Dear Dr. Haselkorn:

I have had the pleasure of knowing Mr. William Smith for about two years. Initially we became acquainted through his interest in my English and Japanese technical communication lectures at Japanese companies. Recently, we have been exchanging our ideas and materials relating to technical communication.

Mr. Smith is highly intelligent, and particularly insightful with regard to the problems of the Japanese technical writer. This I have seen, most recently for example, in the computer manual course he developed and taught at ABC Software.

I recommend without hesitation Mr. Smith's admission to the Master's Program in Scientific and Technical Communication at the ABC University.

Yours sincerely,

【注】日本の英語の先生がアメリカ人を推薦する手紙の例。became acquainted through his interest in ～「彼の～に関心を抱いていたことから知り合った」。insightful「洞察力のある」。

13.9.2 推薦状

通常，様式を守りながら次の項目を書く。

① 提出先の人名が分かれば，普通の Dear Mr.~: か Dear Professor~: で始めるが，分からないときの Salutation は，前述のように To Whom It May Concern: で始めるよりは Dear Director: とか Dear Program Coodinator: などで始めると無味乾燥でなくなる。

② 目的を述べる。

③ どのようにして知り合い，知り合ってから何年になるかを述べる。

④ 志願者，求職者の長所を述べる。

⑤ 志願者，求職者の将来性を述べる。

⑥ 人称代名詞は出来る限り避け，被推薦者の名前を何度も書いて相手に印象づける。

⑦ I strongly recommend that ~ . や I recommend without hesitation ~ . で終える。

13.9.2.1 例文

[Sample letter 48]

Dear Dr. Vasquez:

It is a pleasure to provide a letter of reference for Mr. Taro Suzuki. I had him as a student in my Freshman English class three years ago and know him well.

Mr. Suzuki was a determined and dedicated student, with an interest in language, culture, and international relations that set him apart from his classmates. His pursuit of these interests, both in the classroom and in campus associations, gives firm evidence of his ability to succeed in his postgraduate studies. I have no doubt that he is capable of this program he has applied for.

Mr. Suzuki has a pleasing personality, is outgoing, and works well with others. As he has sought opportunities while at Heisei University to associate with students from other countries, I feel confident that he will get along well with the other members of your academic community and make a positive contribution to it.

I recommend without hesitation Mr. Suzuki's admission to the Masters Program in Communication at the University of ABC.

Yours sincerely,

【注】It is a pleasure to は I am pleased to や I am delighted to より形式ばった堅苦しい Softener。a letter of reference「紹介状」。determined「(性格が) しっかりとした」。dedicated「献身的な；(目的に) ひたむきな」。set him apart from his classmates「彼を他のクラスメートから異にする」。campus associations「学内での交際」。gives firm evidence of ～「～についての確固たる証拠を与える」。
postgraduate studies「大学院での研究 (米では単に graduate という)」。outgoing「積極的な」。he has sought opportunities「彼は機会を探してきた」。while at Heisei University「平成大学の学生の間」。I feel confident that ～「～に確信がある」。get along well with～「と巧くやって行く」。academic community「学園という社会」。positive contribution「明確な貢献」。without hesitation「心から；躊躇なく」。I recommend without hesitation Mr. Suzuki's admission ～ は I strongly recommend that you accept Mr. Suzuki. でもよい。

[Sample letter 49]

Dear Director:

It is a pleasure to recommend Ms. Takeko Yamada for the Master of Communication at Department of Commerce.

I got to know Ms. Takeko Yamada well during the five years she attended my class in English Reading for Sophomores. During her junior and senior years, she belonged to my Advanced Business Communication seminar. And during her postgraduate years, she worked in my office as a teacher's assistant. She was an attentive and devoted student, consistently producing superior work as her scholastic record attests. Ms. Yamada is a positive, outgoing person who works well with others.

Her achievements since her graduate days are impressive. In 1995, she participated in a summer seminar in Communication for Japanese Students at the University of Napoleon. In 1997-98 academic year she attended my graduate course of English Communication at Heisei University. In 1998, she earned a scholarship with honors from the Heian Extension Center for participation in a summer seminar in English Communication at the University of Napoleon.

For these reasons, I have no doubt that Ms. Yamada is qualified for the program she has applied for. I strongly recommend that you accept her.

Sincerely yours,

【注】It is a pleasure to recommend は格式ばった表現。postgraduate years「大学院生（のころ）」。attentive「細やかな気配りをする」。devoted「献身的な」。her scholastic record attests「彼女の成績が証明する」。impressive「見事である」。earned a scholarship]「奨学金を得た」。with honors 「栄誉を得て；優秀のため」。is qualified for ～「～に資格がある；に適任である」

[Sample letter 50]

It is my great pleasure to recommend Mr. Noriaki Iwai for your postgraduate program. I was fortunate to have Mr. Iwai in my seminar on Business and Technical Communication for his junior and senior years in 1996 and 1997. The main objective of my seminar is to provide various ways of communication in English in the business scene, through which I expect that students will cultivate their abilities of research and logical thinking. Mr. Iwai obtained a high evaluation for his research and studies.

In my seminar, everyone is required to make at least one presentation every semester. I clearly remember that the presentation made by Mr. Iwai was very organized and properly analyzed. In addition, his explanation was quite concise and understandable with an effective usage of supplementary tools such as hand-outs, overhead projector, and video. Throughout his presentation, I found that his ability to research and to think logically, which I had concentrated on during the seminar, was quite distinctive.

Mr. Iwai's thesis for my seminar, "The Effective Way of Writing Business Letters," was very impressive. As the title shows, he explained how to write an effective business letters. Once again, he demonstrated his knowledge and ability to use logical thinking. I distinctively remember his remarks in the preface that a message without logic may give rise to misunderstanding. Here he was focused on the importance of conciseness, consistency, and clearness.

I would like to mention also his interest and curiosity in international matters through communication in English. His English was quite impressive although he had never lived abroad, and his eagerness in learning English, getting to know international matters was unparalleled. When I heard he changed jobs from a Japanese manufacturing company to an English reinsuruance company in 1999, I felt he was still as energetic as ever.

I believe that the opportunity for Mr. Iwai to study in your postgraduate program will enhance his already impressive knowledge. I am aware that attending a postgraduate course is a goal that Mr. Iwai has had for many years. Furthermore, I am sure that he is a qualified and talented person who can contribute to your postgraduate program in a variety of ways. Therefore I strongly recommend that you accept his application.

Very truly yours,

【注】It is my great pleasure to は形式ばった表現。cultivate「深める」。was very organized and properly analyzed「よく整理され、分析されていた」。supplementary tools「補助教材」。hand-outs「プリント」プリントは和製英語。distinctive「非凡な」。give rise to ～「～を生

じさせる」。unparalleled「比類が無い」。postgraduate「大学院の」。enhance「高める」

13.10　英文履歴書

　英語では履歴書を，通常，Resume [米] とか Personal History [英] というが，正式には Curriculum Vitae (略してVitae) という。Resume の e に [´] (アクサン) は付けなくてよい。

　英米には市販の履歴書はないので自分でタイプして作る。記載する項目は，Name (氏名)，Address (住所)，Education (学歴)，Work Experience (職歴)，Teaching Experience (教歴)，References (照会者) などである。作成日も As of July 2000 (2000年7月現在) と書く。

　自分を売るために書くのが履歴書だから，Special Talents (特技) やアルバイト (普通は Work Experience の項に書く) まで書く人が多い。

　個人的に干渉されるのを嫌う人は，Date of Birth (生年月日)，Age (年齢)，Family (既婚，未婚，家族) などは書かなくてよい。アメリカでは書かない傾向が強い。

　日本の履歴書の「賞罰なし (Rewards and Punishments: None) とか「右相違ありません (I declare that the above statement is correct and true.) は英語の履歴書では書かない。

　学歴や職歴は日本と異なり，新しいものから古いものへの順に書くのが普通である。

[例]　1990-1993　Attended Heisei University as a Research Student in the graduate level of the Department of Literature, where I studied Modern American Literature. (平成大学で大学院の研究生として文学部へ在籍し，現代アメリカ文学を研究)

　　　1987-1990　Graduated from Toyoko University with an M.A. in Oriental Languages and Korean Language. (東横大学文学部修士課程修了。東洋言語と韓国語を研究)

　Special Talents (特技) の項には Fluent Spoken English (英会話流暢) のように書く。Special Talents の代わりに Special Attributes and

Personality として Feel at home in an American environment. Am able to communicate effectively and easily with American clients (アメリカの環境に順応性あり。アメリカの顧客と効果的にスムースに意志の伝達可) と書いたり，Foreign Travel and Experience (外国旅行と経験) の項を設け，Okinawa — 1985, USA — 1986のように書いて，終えてもよい。

13.10.1 自分を売込む手紙の例

日本では，自分のことは，謙遜して，控えめに言ったり，書いたりするのが普通だが，欧米では逆で，できる限りこの機会に自分を売り込もうと努める習慣がある。

[Sample letter 51]

<u>Sending Curriculum Vitae</u>

Dear Director:

In response to your requirement, I am enclosing my resume.

Can your business use a soon-to-be-graduated student who can handle things practically? Who is fluent in English? Who is an energetic person? If "Yes" is your answer, then I may be the very person you are looking for.

As I mentioned in the enclosed resume, I go to Waseda University, School of Commerce, especially studying Advanced Business Communication. As I mainly study English documents in the seminar, I believe my skill in writing effective documents will be helpful when I work for you. In addition, I have taken classes of Securities,

Finance, Commercial Law, and so on. I am sure that the knowledge of these will also be useful in your company.

I am looking for a position in which I will be able to use my skills and, at the same time, develop my potentials.

I am, therefore, extremely interested in holding a position in your investment banking business, for it seems to be a very responsible and influential business in society.

As you have a global network, principally in New York and London, and good know-how of course, I think working as a member of your company means working for the world's best securities company. I am one who would like to work for a professional team like yours.

Thank you for your consideration, and I am very much looking forward to seeing you again.

Sincerely yours,

Enclosure: Resume and Self-introduction sheet

> 【注】「履歴書」に対する形式ばった言い方が Curriculum Vitae で、通常は、Vitae とか Resume という。Personal History は英国で多用される。in response to~ (~のご返事として) はよく使われる。response は answer よりも形式ばった語。
> 第二パラグラフでは疑問文を使って、自分が貴社に正しくうってつけの人物であると宣伝している。soon-to-be-graduated「まもなく卒業する」
> 第三パラグラフでは自分が大学で履修した科目をあげながら、自分の能力を売っている。Securities「証券論」, Finance「金融論」, Commercial Law「商法」
> 第四パラグラフでは第三パラグラフで説明した能力を活かしたいと必至になっていることが理解できる。potentials「可能性；潜在能力」

第五パラグラフでは自分の働きたい仕事を明確に述べている。hold a position「職につく」。position は job より形式ばった語。investment banking「投資銀行の」。responsible「責任のある」。influential「重要な（役割を果たす）」

第六パラグラフでは就職希望の会社を褒め，貴社のような世界的に有名な企業で働きたいと意志表示をしている。就職希望の会社を褒めることが大切。global network「世界中のネットワーク」。know-how「専門的知識」。securities company「証券会社」

第七パラグラフでは，最終段階で「私を斟酌（考慮）していただき有り難うございました」だけではなく，「もう一度是非お会いできることを楽しみにしています」と確信をほのめかしながら結んでいる。なお，I am looking forward to と進行形を使って強調している。

13.10.2 履歴書の例

[Sample 52]

RESUME

Tomoko Ohno
3-36-11 Kita-machi
Setagaya-ku, Tokyo 158-0000
Phone: 03-555-8888
email: shino@prs.takeya.net.jp

Personal Data	Date of Birth	July 1, 1975
	Sex	Female
	Marital States	Single
Education	April 1994 to present	Student, School of Commerce, Waseda University, Shinjuku, Tokyo B. C., March 1998
	April 1991-March 1994	Sakura High School, Chofu, Tokyo

Qualifications	Passed STEP, Pre-First, July 1993
	Received driver's license, July 1994
	Passed BETA Level 3, January 1997
	Took TOEIC 900 points, January 1997
	Passed TEP Test 2nd Class, May 1998

Other Information	1997	Special study: Advanced Business Communication, Waseda University
	1996	Attended 2 weeks' Business and Technical Communication summer seminar, University of Michigan
	1991	3-month experience staying with an American family as an exchange student in Michigan, USA

References	Available upon request

13.11　冠婚葬祭の英語

　冠婚葬祭は國により習慣を異にする。カードや手紙を用いるのが普通だが文面も国や宗教により異なるので注意しよう。欧米では封筒付きで，様々な内容の英文が印刷されたカードを，本屋や日用雑貨店でたくさん売っている。このようなカードを利用するときは，通常はカードに一筆したため，サインをして封筒に入れて出すのが普通である。

13.11.1　注意事項

　「幸せ」の手紙は遅くなってからでもよいが，「不幸」の手紙は速やかに出すべきである。

I sympathize with you about your father's death.

(ご尊父様のご逝去をお悔み申し上げます)

お見舞状には,

Get well quickly!（早くよくなってね)

などに加えて,

Lick that germ!（そんな病原菌など負かしてね)

とか,

Good luck!（頑張れよ)

が若い世代向きだろう。

お目出たい場合は，個性が出て，ウイットに富んだ文言がよい。逆に不幸なときは，相手をからかうような軽い文言は避けるべきである。

誕生日を祝うには、

Happy birthday, Tom.

に加えて，親友なら

Don't eat too much cake!（ケーキを食べ過ぎないように)

とか,

You would get a cake with 3 candles on it.

(ろうそくを30本さしたケーキを貰うでしょう)

これは30才になったことを意味する。30本のろうそくケーキにさせないので1本を10才とみて1本といっている。

結婚を祝うときは，少なくとも

Congratulations on your Marriage!（ご結婚おめでとう)

ぐらいは自筆で書く。また,

Very deserving, wonderful couple — you!

(お似合いで，素晴らしいお二人。それはあなた方です)

とか,

May a beautiful wedding day be the perfect beginning of a long life of happiness.

(素晴らしい結婚式の日がこれからの長い人生の幸せの正しく初日でありますように)

ぐらいは書きたいものだ。

　卒業を祝うときは，

　Congratulations, Graduate!（ご卒業おめでとう）

の次に，

　You'll find success and happiness in the years ahead of you.
　（あなたの前途にはご成功とご多幸が待っています）

とか，

　May this really great occasion be only the beginning of many more successes and honors you'll be winning.
　（この本当に偉大な時があなたの将来の数々のご成功と名誉の始まりでありますように）

のような大袈裟な表現が好まれる。

　お礼状には，少なくとも、

　Thank you very much!

とか，

　The memories will last a lifetime.
　（この思い出は一生忘れません）

とか，

　Thank you a million for the birthday gift, John!
　（ジョン，誕生日の贈り物本当に有り難う）

ぐらいは書きたい。

　You are so thoughtful!（あなたは本当に思いやりがあります）

も多用されている。もてなしを受けたならば，

　Your hospitality was so much appreciated.
　（あなたのおもてなしに厚く御礼申し上げます）

とやや堅苦しい言い方もある。

13.11.2　お悔やみ状

[Sample letter 53]

Dear Smith:

I was saddened to learn that your mother passed away recently. Having suffered the loss of my parents, I know how you feel and can sympathize with you. I hope your sadness will be tempered by many loving memories.

Sincerely,

> 【注】この種の手紙はくどくど書かないこと。againのような単語の使用には注意をする方がよい。「不幸が again（返ってくる）」ような印象を与えることがあるからだ。passed away（他界した）はdied（死んだ）の遠まわしな表現。sympathize with you（お悔やみ申し上げる，心中をお察しする）。I sympathize with you about your mother's death.（ご母堂様のご逝去をお悔やみ申し上げます）のように用いる。be tempered by 〜「〜によって和らげられる」

[Sample letter 54]

Dear Smith:

I was sorry to hear of your father's death. My thoughts and prayers are with you at this very trying time.
Since I live so far away, I cannot, unfortunately, attend the funeral services, but I will certainly pray for Mr. Smith. May God bless you and your family with the strength to bear this heavy burden.

Sincerely,

【注】 My thoughts and prayers are with you at this very trying time. は「心からお悔やみ申し上げます。お気を落としになりませぬように」に当たる。Trying「苦しい，つらい」。pray for「（ご冥福）を祈る」。May God bless you and your family with the strength「あなたとご家族の皆様に神のご加護をお祈りいたします」。to bear this heavy burden「この大きい悲しみに耐えられる」。

13.11.3 Christmas Card

外国にはいろいろ異なるな宗教があり，宗教により文面が異なるので注意。クリスマス　カードは既製のものを利用してよいが，クリスチャンでない人に Merry Christmas と書いたカードは送らないほうが安全。クリスチャンか否かの見分けかたは相手からきたクリスマスカードにMerry Christmas が書いてなければクリスチャンではないのが普通である。

ごく一般的な英文はすでに印刷してあっても、年号と Salutation と結びの英語は必ず手書きにする。

[Sample 55]

A New Year Wish
ACROSS THE MILES

【注】 文面が印刷されている簡単なクリスマス・カードの例。印刷した英文に次のような簡単な近況を添えると暖かさがでて，こちらの気持ちが伝わるだろ。

Dear Tom,

Mary and I hope the new year finds you and your family are good health. The holidays are always a very busy time for my job and this year is no exception.

このような文に家族の近況を添えるのが普通である。

[Sample 56]

With wishes for a year of good luck, health, and every happiness.
> 【注】 good luck, health, and every happiness（ご幸運と，ご健康と，ご多幸）のように3つ並べるのが習慣である。この次に家族などの近況を続けるのが普通である。

類例として次のような英文もある。

[Sample 57]

Best Wishes for Peace and Joy this Holiday Season and a New Year of Health, Happiness and Prosperity.
> 【注】 Holiday Season までは決まった表現。これ以下は「新しい年が，ご健康と，ご多幸と，ご繁栄の年でありますように」のこと。

[Sample 58]

The Season's Greeting with best wishes for your happiness in the New Year
> 【注】 これに近況を添えるのが普通である。

[Sample 59]

Dear friends,
Merry Christmas
and a Happy New Year
and may God's blessing be with you
throughout the year
      With our love,
       （サイン）

【注】クリスチャンからの例。Merry Christmas and a Happy New Year は印刷してあり，他の英文はペンの直筆が添えてあった。and may God's blessing be with you throughout the year は With my love and best wishes for the coming year でもよい。なお日付も Christmas 2000 のように書くのを忘れないように。

[Sample 60]

Dear Mike,

I hope you are enjoying the vacation even if you are still very busy with other work and activities!

I do appreciate all the nice things you have done while I was in New York. Thank you. My best wishes for the holidays.

Takeo

[Sample 61]

文面が印刷してあるカードに添える文として，次のような例がある。
* My best wishes to you for a happy 20xx.
* All the best for the New Year.
* Warmest best wishes for the holiday season!
* Warmest best wishes to you and your family for 20xx.
* Happy New Year—health and happiness to you.
* I hope you enjoy a wonderful holiday season.
* May you have a Merry Christmas and a Happy New Year.
* Best wishes for the holidays and the coming year.
* Best wishes to you all for a happy Christmas and a joyful New Year
* May your Christmas be a happy one and your New Year a prosperous one.
* Merry Christmas, Tom! May the New Year be a good one for you.
* Merry Christmas! Best wishes from everyone in our house to every-

one in yours.
* Pray that the suffering in many parts of the world does not touch you.
* Do hope you and your family had a great 2001 with good health. The best of everything in 2002.［Do hope は I do hope のこと］
* Although Christmas isn't a holiday here as it is in your country, we'll be remembering you and other good friends. Happy New Year!
* We send our best wishes for a happy holiday season and every success in the New Year.（企業などが出す例）
* I hope 20XX will be pleasant and prosperous for you.
* Hope all is well with you! Best wishes for the new year!
* Wishing you everything wonderful of this special Holiday Season and always. (この種の英文はよく印刷されている)
* May the beauty of Christmas brighten all the year for you. Best wishes for a pleasant holiday season.
* Wishing you Peace, Joy and Contentment
* Wishing you the very best during the holidays and throughout the new year. Have a wonderful, healthy 20XX.
* We're both wishing you a Christmas
    as warm as the glow
    of holiday candles,
    as delightful as the first snowfall,
    as wonderful as the good times
    shared with friends.
  Merry Christmas from both,
    （夫婦のサイン）
* May the miracles of Christmas fill your heart with joy and peace.
  With our love,
    （夫婦のサイン）

13.11.4　Valentine Day

Valentine's Day はアメリカやイギリスでは日本のように派手ではないが，次のような文面のカードを送るようだ。

[Sample 62]

The wish that's in	このヴァレンタインデーのカードに
this Valentine's Day card	こめた願いは
is for today, it's true,	今日のためであることは当然ですが
but the love	このカードがもたらす
and warmth it's bringing	愛と熱い思いは
are for now and always too!	今だけでなく，永遠なり！
Happy Valentine's Day	ハッピーヴァレンタインデー

【注】　この種の手紙は形式だけのものが多い。この例もありふれた文面のカードといえよう。true と too が韻を踏んでいる。Happy Valentine's Day だけでよいものに上の6行は付け足したもの。

第14章

参考

14.1 世界各国の貨幣単位 (Monetary Units)

国別 (country), 基本単位 (basic unit), 標準補助 (standard subdivision), 符号 (symbol) の順に挙げる。

Standard

Country	Basic Unit	Subdivision	Symbol
Afghanistan	afghani	100 puls	Af.
Albania	lek	100 quintars	L
Algeria	dinar	100 centimes	DA
Andorra	franc	100 centimes	Fr. F
Angola	kwanza	100 lwei	Kz
Antigua and Barbuda	dollar	100 cents	AB $
Argentina	peso	100 centavos	a $
Australia	dollar	100 cents	A $
Austria*	schilling	100 groschen	S
Bahamas	dollar	100 cents	$B
Bahrain	dinar	100 fils	BD
Bangladesh	taka	100 paise	T
Barbados	dollar	100 cents	$B
Belgium*	franc	100 centimes	BF
Belize	dollar	100 cents	$B
Benin	CFA franc	100 centimes	CFAF
Bolivia	boliviano	100 centavos	Bs
Brazil	real	100 centavos	real
Bulgaria	lev	100 stotinki	LV
Burkina Faso	CFA franc	100 centimes	CFAF

Burundi	franc	100 centimes	Fbu
Cameroun	CFA franc	100 centimes	CFAF
Canada	dollar	100 cents	C$
Central African Republic	CFA franc	100 centimes	CFAF
Chad	CFA franc	100 centimes	CFAF
Chile	peso	100 centavos	peso
China	yuan	100 fen	Yuan
Colombia	peso	100 centavos	Col$
Congo, the People's Republic of the	CFAF franc	100 centimes	CFAF
Costa Rica	colon	100 centimos	¢
Côte d'Ivoire	CFA franc	100 centimes	CFAF
Cyprus	pound	100 cents	LC
Czech Republic	koruna	100 halers	Kc
Denmark	krone	100 øre	DKr
Dominican Republic	peso	100 centavos	RD$
Ecuador	sucre	100 centavos	S/
Egypt	pound	100 piasters	LE
El Salvador	colon	100 centavos	¢
Equatorial Guinea	CFA franc	100 centimes	CFAF
Finland*	markka	100 pennia	Fmk
France*	franc	100 centimes	Fr
Gabon	CFA franc	100 centimes	CFAF
Gambia	dalasi	100 butut	LG
Germany*	mark	100 pfennig	DM
Ghana	cedi	100 pesewa	N¢
Greece	drachma	100 lepta	Dr
Guatemala	quetzal	100 centavos	Q
Guyana	dollar	100 cents	G$
Haiti	gourde	100 centimes	G$

Honduras	lempira	100 centavos	L
Hungary	forint	100 filler	Ft
Iceland	krona	100 filler	Ft
India	rupee	100 paise	R
Indonesia	rupiah	100 sen	Rp
Iran	rial	100 dinars	RI
Iraq	dinar	1000 fils	ID
Ireland, the Republic of * (*or* the Irish Republic)	punt	100 pence	Llr.
Israel	shekel	100 agorot	1L
Italy*	lira	100 centesmi	Lit
Jamaica	dollar	100 cents	J$
Japan	yen	100 sen	¥
Jordan	dinar	1000 fils	JD
Kenya	shilling	100 cents	K Sh.
Kuwait	dinar	1000 fils	KD
Laos	kip	100 at	K
Lebanon	pound	100 piasters	LL
Lesotho	loti	100 lisente	L
Liberia	dollar	100 cents	S
Libya	dinar	100 dirhams	Din
Luxembourg*	franc	100 centimes	Lux. F
Malagasy Republic	franc	100 centimes	FMG
Malawi, Republic of	kwacha	100 tambala	KW
Malaysia	ringgit	100 sen	MS
Mali	CFA franc	100 centimes	MF
Malta	lira	100 cents	LM
Mauritania	ouguiya	5 khoums	Oug
Mauritius	rupee	100 cents	MRp
Mexico	peso	100 centavos	Mex$

Country	Currency	Subunit	Symbol
Mongolia, the Mongolian People's Republic	tugrik	100 mongos	Tu
Morocco	dirham	100 centimes	DH
Nepal	rupee	100 paise	NR
Netherlands*	guilder	100 cents	Fls.
New Zealand	dollar	100 cents	NZ$
Nicaragua	cordoba	100 centavos	C$
Niger	franc	100 centimes	CFAF
Nigeria	naira	100 kobo	N
North Korea	won	100 jun	W
Norway	krone	100 øre	NKr
Oman	rial	1000 baiza	RS
Pakistan	rupee	100 paisa	PR
Panama	balboa	100 centesimos	B
Philippines, the Republic of the,	peso	100 centavos	Esc
Poland	zloty	100 groszy	Zl
Portugal*	escudo	100 centavos	Esc
Qatar	riyal	100 dirhams	R
Romania	leu	100 bani	L
Rwanda	franc	100 centimes	CFAF
Saudi Arabia	riyal	100 halalas	SRl
Senegal	franc	100 centimes	CFAF
Sierra Leone	leone	100 cents	Le
Singapore	dollar	100 cents	S$
Somali Democratic Republic	shilling	100 cents	So.Sh
South Korea	won	100 chon	W
Spain*	peseta	100 centimos	Pta or Pts (*pl*)
Sri Lanka	rupee	100 cents	Cey R

Sudan	dinar	10 pounds	SdL
Suriname	guilder	100 cents	Sur. Fls
Switzerland	franc	100 centimes	SFr
Syria	pound	100 piasters	SL
Taiwan	dollar	100 cents	NT$
Tanzania	shilling	100 cents	T. Sh.
Thailand	bath	100 satangs	B
Togo	franc	100 centimes	CFAF
Tonga	pa'anga	100 seniti	なし
Trinidad and Tobago	dollar	100 cents	TT$
Tunisia	dinar	1000 millimes	D
Turkey	lira	100 kurus	TL
Uganda	shilling	100 cents	U. Sh.
United Kingdom	pound	100 pence	£
United States of America	dollar	100 cents	$
Uruguay	peso	100 centimos	UR$
Uzbekistan	sum	なし	なし
Venezuela	bolivar	100 centimos	B
Vietnam	dong	10 hao/100 xu	D
Yemen	rial	100 fils	R
Yugoslavia	dinar	100 paras	Din
Zambia	kwacha	100 ngwee	KW
Zimbabwe	dollar	100 cents	Z$

＊2001年1月より通貨をeuroに換える。

(J.F.Buschini & R. R. Reynolds: *Communication in Business*, Houghton Mifflin Company, Massachusetts, USA と T. Matsuda:*Kenkyusha's English-Japanese Dictionary for the General Reader*, Second Edition, Kenkyusha, Tokyo などによる)

14.2 数字による各国の日付表示法

算用数字で日付を表示すると年，月，日の順序が国により異なる。ここでは February 15, 2001 を例として表してみたい。

Arabic countries	01/02/15
Australia	15/2/01
Austria	15.2.2001
Bulgaria	2001-II-15
Canada (English)	15/02/01
Canada (French)	2001-02-15
China	15/2/01（または2001.02.15）
France	15/02/2001
Indonesia	15/2/01
Japan	2001-02-15
Korea	2001.02.15
Malaysia	15/2/01
New Zealand	15/2/01
The Philippines	2/15/01
Singapore	15/2/01
Taiwan	01/02/15
Thailand	15/2/01
United Kingdom	15/02/01
USA	02/15/01（軍隊は 15/02/01）
Vietnam	15/2/01

このように，国によって異なるので，算用数字だけで表記すると誤解される恐れがでてくる。したがって，次のいずれかを用いると受信者は間違いなく理解できる。

February 15, 2001	2001 February 15
Feb. 15, 2001	2001-February-15

15 February 2001

標準の米用法はFebruary 15, 2001であり，軍隊では，15 February 2001が普通である。(*IBM National Language Support Reference Manual*, Fourth Edition参考)

14.3 国際電話の国番号

Country	Telephone number	Country	Telephone number
Albania	355	Croatia	385
Algeria	213	Cuba	53
Argentina	54	Czech Republic	420
Armenia	374	Denmark	45
Australia	61	Egypt	20
Austria	43	Estonia	372
Bahrain	973	Ethiopia	251
Bangladesh	880	Fiji	679
Belarus	375	Finland	358
Belgium	32	France	33
Bosnia and Herzegovina	387	Georgia	995
Brazil	55	Germany	49
Brunei	673	Greece	30
Bulgaria	359	Hong Kong	852
Cambodia	855	Hungary	36
Canada	1	India	91
Chile	56	Indonesia	62
China	86	Iran	98
Colombia	57	Iraq	964
Costa Rica	506	Ireland	353
Cote d' Ivoire	225	Israel	972

Italy	39	Philippines	63
Jamaica	1	Poland	48
Japan	81	Portugal	351
Jordan	962	Qatar	974
Kazakhstan	7	Russian Federation	7
Kenya	254	Saudi Arabia	966
Kuwait	965	Singapore	65
Laos	856	Slovakia	421
Latvia	371	Slovenia	386
Lebanon	961	South Africa	27
Liberia	231	South Korea	82
Lithuania	370	Spain	34
Malaysia	60	Sri Lanka	94
Mexico	52	Sudan	249
Monaco	377	Sweden	46
Mongolia	976	Switzerland	41
Morocco	212	Taiwan	886
Myanmar	95	Tanzania	255
Nepal	977	Thailand	66
Netherlands	31	Tunisia	216
New Zealand	64	Turkey	90
Nigeria	234	Ukraine	380
North Korea	850	United Arab Emirates	971
Norway	47	United Kingdom	44
Oman	968	United States America	1
Pakistan	92	Venezuela	58
Panama	507	Vietnam	84
Papua New Guinea	675	Yemen	967
Paraguay	595	Yugoslavia	381
Peru	51		

和文索引

【あ】

愛顧	
挨拶	171
挨拶文句	41
相槌	164
悪印象	166
頭にくる	164
斡旋	121
宛先	58,136
後払い法	112
アドレス	139
アブストラクト	145
アメリカ英語	45
アルバイト	182
案内状	55

【い】

Eメール	140
怒る	168
イギリス英語	45
以上	73
委託番号	15
一覧払	82
一括提案	159
一手代理店	89
一手販売代理店	86,102
一手販売権契約	87
一手販売店	75,86
印刷物	58,88,93
インターネット	140,141
インボイス	117

【う】

ヴァレンタインデー	194
受取船荷証券	105
打消し	19
写しの送付先	52
売りオファー	77
売込む	183
売違い御免オファー	78
売申込み	70,75
運送	95
運送書類	111
運送費用	117
運賃・保険料込み価格	107
運賃込み価格	106
運賃込み値段	123
運賃支払済み	107
運賃着払い	104
運賃・保険料込み渡し	117
運賃保険料支払済み	107
運賃前払済み	104

【え】

営業状態	22,64
衛生証明書	105
遠慮なく~する	76

【お】

応答	158
沖仲士	103
送り状	104,117
送る	14,20
脅す	162
オファー	14,77,78,83
折返し	99
折り返し航空便	90
折込み印刷物	88

お礼状	127
卸売値段表	126

【か】

買いオファー	77
海外販売代理店	86
外貨資金割当	103
会議	152,153,155
開催日	154
会社	65,130
海上損害	106
海上保険証券	104
開設	112
開設する	97
改善する	26
買付代理店	86
開店披露状	125
回答期限	77
解約	120
買約書	83
海洋運賃	119
街路名	37
格式張り	145
確認銀行	113
確認信用状	112
カウンター・オファー	83
家屋番号	37
価格	61,78
書留	58
格式張る	12
確定オファー	77,78
確認条件付きオファー	77,78
確定注文；期限指定注文	75
学歴	182
掛け売り（勘定）	115
掛け勘定	117
箇条書	66,67
貸す	14

肩書き	39,43,47,153,155,156
カタログ	71,73
カタログ在中	58
カバーシート	133
貨幣単位	195
貨物の損傷	120
仮送り状	117
仮予約	108
為替手形	82,104,112
関係代名詞	23
冠婚葬祭	186
勘定	98
感情アイコン	141
勘定書	115
勘定につける	99
簡略型	56

【き】

期限付き	111
記号	141,142
既婚	48,182
議事	153,155
議事録	22,151,153,154,155,156
技術上の目的	147
規則	117
議題	153,157,15
議長	158,159
議長名	152,153,155
気付け	49
義務	29
疑問文	166
記名式船荷証券	105
記録者名	152
逆オファー	83,95
キャンペーン	73
求償	120
求職者	177
協会貨物約款	106

協議事項	153	減価償却	68
共同海損	106	検査証明書	105
教歴	182	現実全損	106
議論	157	謙譲語	12
銀行	112	件名欄	50
		権利	87

【く】

空港渡し	106		
空輸	13,20		
苦情	15,20,26,120,121		

【こ】

句読点厳守型	57	厚意	20
句読点混合型	57	航海の遅延	100
句読点省略型	57	好感	166
句読法	24,57	抗議	171
悔やみ状	189	航空貨物運送状	105
クリスマスカード	190	航空便	58
クレーム	120,121	控除	117
クレッジット	94	好評	148
		効力	115

【け】

敬具	46	口語調	12,13
敬語	12	口語表現	140
敬称	36,39,41,42,43,52155,156	工場渡し価格	106
携帯電話	13	肯定	19
契約	77,78,82,95,100,105	公文書	34
契約期間	87	広報部	132
契約書	28,87,95,99	考慮する	14
契約書調	26	国際電話番号	201
契約不履行	120	国際標準図書番号	98
形容詞	18	故障	17
決議	152	故障船荷証券	105
結婚	187	個人攻撃	170
決済;清算	117	個人名	41,42
欠席者名	152	語調	12,14,70,90,126,165,167
結論	145,147	小包	13
決定事項	156	コロン	41,42
けなす	162	梱包方法	62
県	45	コンマ	37,41,42

【さ】

財政状態	63
サイン	47,136,146
最終確認	80
先売り	82
先売り御免オファー	78
作成日	182
避けたい語	30
指図式船荷証券	105
差出人住所	44,58
差別語	29,103
差別主義者	42
散会	160
参考	80,88,96
参考文献	145
参照番号	119
参照欄	49
残高	114
賛否	156

【し】

市	37,45
志願者	177
市・区・町	37
仕向地	110
試算用送り状	117
下取り	75
質問	172
指定倉庫渡し価格	106
支店	126
品違い	120
老舗	15
支払い	94,98,111
支払条件	62,82
支払方法	61,95
支払渡し手形	111
事務局長	132
写真在中	58

社内連絡状	146
社名	33,36,39,65,154
州名	37,39,41
終了時間	152
受益者	113
重要項目	45
主題	31,32,45,139
首題	31,50,66
受諾	95
出荷	117
出荷案内	104
出荷案内書	104
出荷する	26
出港許可書	117
出席者	152
出席者名	155
受動態	21,22
種目	80
受領者が二人	43
私用	34
仕様変更	148
照会者	182
商業送り状	104,105
商業会議所	64
商業興信所	115
条件	73,96
条件付き	77
条項	87
商工会議所	64
小冊子	15
賞賛	162
訴訟	121
招待状	55
承諾	77,83
譲渡可能	105
譲渡可能信用状	112
譲渡できない	110

和文索引

常任委員会	154
承認状	104,105
賞罰なし	182
消費者	148
商品	13,78
初回金	82
職歴	182
書状内宛名	36
序数	45
助動詞	26,27
署名	47,134,135,146
審議	156
申請	84
人名	39
人物紹介状	174
信用状	94,104,109,112,114
信用状態	22,64
信用譲与会社	115
信頼性	73

【す】

数量・個数不足	120
推薦	147,159
推薦状	43174,176,177
推定全損	106
数量	61,80,83,95
勧める語	30
スタイル	12,13
スペルアウト	45
スマイリー	141,142

【せ】

姓	41
税関送り状	105
請求書	115
逝去	189
性差別語	103
精算	119

製造物責任	120
生年月日	182
製品	93
積送品	124
セクハラ	29
接続詞	24
7 C's	11
全危険担保	106
全損	106,123

【そ】

相違	182
送金	111
送金為替	112
送信	136
総代理店	86
速達	58
卒業	188
尊敬	14
尊敬語	12

【た】

代案	158
台数	97
タイピスト	51
代表的なサンプル	88
代名詞	29
代理署名	48
代理店	86,88,102
代理店契約	99
立替金	119
ダブルスペース	45
単価	80
男女の区別	36
誕生日	187
単独海損	106

【ち】

遅延	100

遅延状	100,103
仲裁	121
注文	26,29,95,119
注文確認書	83,119
注文書	95
注文承諾書	83
注文する	12,20
注文請書	83
注文払い	112
注文用紙	72
調査	147
調査結果	147
調査研究	129
調査する	28
町名	45
チラシ	88

【つ】

追加	145
追伸	53,65
追追伸	65
通貨	80
通関	104
通関手続	103
通知銀行	112
月	46
都合	91
積出し	104
積出通知	110
積出す	110

【て】

定期的	21
ディストリビューター	86
提出先	177
丁寧語	12
定例会議	154,160
手紙指示事項	58

手数料	87,99
転勤通知状	132
手続き	117
点検売買オファー	78
10C's	11
電子メール	138,139
伝達上の目的	147

【と】

同意	166,167
討議	156
討議事項	156,159
動議	152,156,159
当社	65
投票	159
投票数	156
同封	99
同封する	14
同封物記入欄	51
特技	182
特長	171
特定名宛人欄	49
特別委員会	154
特約店	64
届ける	14
怒鳴る	164
扉	145
取扱銀行	99
取消し可能信用状	112
取消不能信用状	97,112,113
取立状	113
取引関係	173
取引銀行	97,112,119
取引条件	63,77
取引高[量]	88
取引申込状	86

和文索引

【な】
名前　　　　　　　　　39

【に】
荷印　　　　　　　　　95
荷為替　　　　　　　　111
荷為替信用状　　　　　112
荷為替手形　　　　　　104,111
荷造り　　　　　　　　62,95
2ページ目　　　　　　33
日本の手紙　　　　　　45
人称代名詞　　　　　　140,147,177

【ね】
値段　　　　　　　　　29,95,99
値段表　　　　　　　　94
年　　　　　　　　　　46
年齢　　　　　　　　　182

【の】
納期　　　　61,68,78,83,95,100,172
能動態　　　　　　　　21,165
納品　　　　　　　　　20,21,103
納品書　　　　　　　　104

【は】
拝啓　　　　　　　　　41
配達費無料　　　　　　75
売買契約書　　　　　　95
ハイフン　　　　　　　46
売約書　　　　　　　　83,95
発行銀行　　　　　　　113
発表　　　　　　　　　161
幅広い　　　　　　　　15
話し合い　　　　　　　161
パラグラフ　　　　　　32,45
反対　　　　　　　　　167
反対オファー　　　　　83
番地　　　　　　　　　37,39

販売代理店　　　　　　86

【ひ】
引合い　　　　　　　　61,66,70,77
引受渡し手形　　　　　111
ビジネスレター　　　　46
日付　　　　　　　　　33,36
表記(してある)値段　　94
表紙　　　　　　　　　145
品質相違　　　　　　　120
品質不良　　　　　　　120
日付表示　　　　　　　200
品名　　　　　　　　　61
品目　　　　　　　　　80,87,88

【ふ】
ファクシミリ　　　　　11,12
　　　　　　　46,51,56,133,144
ファックス　　　　　　134,135
封筒　　　　　　　　　58,59
不快感　　　　　　　　163
不可抗力　　　　　　　100,109,121
副詞　　　　　　　　　18
複写　　　　　　　　　94
複数の受信人　　　　　37
部署名　　　　　　　　39,42,47
不信感　　　　　　　　162
付帯状況　　　　　　　85
船積み　　　　　　　　100,104
船積小荷物受領証　　　105
船積書類　　　　　　　104
船積船荷証券　　　　　105
船積相違　　　　　　　120
船積遅延　　　　　　　100,120
船積通知　　　　　　　104
船積日　　　　　　　　109
船積不履行　　　　　　120
船荷証券　　　　　　　100,104,105,123

— 209 —

船荷書類	105,112
船便	58,98
不便	102
付録	145
プロフォーマ	117
憤慨	168
文責者	51
分損	106

【へ】

部屋番号	37
返事	82
返送先	44
返品	28

【ほ】

法規違反	120
暴言	162
報告書	23
包装	80
包装不備	120
包装明細書	105
保険	62,95,104
保険証券	105
保険料	105,117
保証	27,113,173
補償	123
保証期間	13,94
保証期限	15
本社	126
本船受取証	111
本船渡し価格	106
本船渡し条件値段	99
本人	86
本文	45,145
本論	145

【ま】

マーケット・クレーム	120

前払い	119
前払い法	112
街表示	40
満場一致	157,159
マンション	44

【み】

ミーティング	153
未婚	48,182
未着	14
見積り送り状	117
未亡人	48
魅力	29

【む】

無確認信用状	113
無効	27
無故障船荷証券	105
結び文句	46
無料	94

【め】

冥福	190
メーカー	17,65
銘柄	95
明記	20
明細	61,96
明白	147
免税証明書類	75

【も】

申込み	77,86
目次	145
目的	28,31,32,147
問題提起法	148
問題点	148
問題解決	162

【ゆ】

有効期間	119

有効期限	77,109,119
郵便小包受領証	105
郵便 為替	115
郵便番号	39
輸出港船側渡し価格	106
輸出承認	117
輸出代理店	86
輸出品	93
輸送費用	117
輸入承認	117

【よ】

要求	13,14,19
容積重量証明書	105
様式	54,57
横浜港運賃込み渡し	117
予定日時	159
予約	104

【り】

略語	36,37,39,41,140,141,151
量	97
領事送り状	105
履歴書	182,184

【れ】

レターペーパー	33,58,59
レターヘッド	34
レンタル品	126

【わ】

和解	121
割引	73

英 文 索 引

【A】

Absent	155
Abstract	145
account	114,115
acceptance	77,78,83,95,148
Acceptance of Order	83
Acknowledgment of Order	83
Actual Total Loss	106
Ad hoc Committee	154
Address	57,139,182
adjourn	160
adjournment	160,152
adjustment	118,119
advance	118,119,141
advantage	150,151,171,172
advertisement	62,71
Advising Bank	112
AFAIK	141
afraid	14,15
Agent, agent	86,88,89,90,91,101
agree	164,166,167
agreement	167
Air Mail	58
Air Waybill	105
airfreight	13
airmail	16,20
All Risks	106
alley	17,18
allocation	103
alternative	158
Amendment	123
amicable settlement	121
amount	23
analysis	149,151
Analytic Report	145
angry	168
apologize	74,75,76,101,102,103,137
Appendix	145
Application	84
appreciate	13,64,69,90,98,103,166
approval	147
arbitration	121
As ever,	46
as of	101,102,114,115
as per	108,109,118
assignment	131
assistance	127
association	127
assume	23
assure	63,115
Attendance	155
Attention,attention	49,50,98
Attention Line	49
Attn	35, 49,101
attractive	29
automobile	17
available	18,63,64,74,75
avenue	17
awful	18

【B】

B/L	105,109,122,123
back	141
backlog	101,102
bad packing	120
balance due	114
bank	62,63,81,82,98

banker	97	C & F	105,106,107
BBL	141	calm	164,168,171
bcc	53	can	27,28,30
beautiful	166	cancellation	120
behalf	137	Candid	11
believe	94,110	cannot	20
Beneficiary	113	car	17
best regards	130,139	Carbon Copy Notation	52
Best wishes, best wishes		case	137
	46,132,192,193	cash	92
bet	173	Cash on Shipment	111
Bibliography	145	Cash with Order	112
Bill of Exchange	112	catalog	68,69,71,72,73,75,76
Bill of Lading, bill of lading		Catalog Only	58
	100,104,105,123	CAUTION	121
birthday	187,188	CC, cc	35,52,53
Blank Paper	33	cellular phone	13
Block Style	54,55,57	Certificate	104,105
board	109	Certificate and List of Measurement	
Body	145,147	and / or Weight	105
Body of Letter	45	CFR	105,106,116,117,122,123
Body Proper	145	chairperson	154,155,158,159,160
booking	104	charge	94,97,98,99,123,124
booklets	15	charge account	115
boulevard	17	cheap	166
branch	125,126	check	23,27
breach of contract	120	Cheers	46
brochure	65	choose	16
BTW	141	Christmas Card	190
buy	16	CIF	82,96,99,104,105,107
buyer	85,96	circular	92
buying agent	86	city	37
Buying Offer	77	claim	19,120,122
By	48	Clarity	11
Bye	139	Clean B/L	105
		Clear, clear	11,101
【C】		Clearness	11
C.I.F.	117	Closed-Punctuation Pattern	57

Closing	46,134,146	Consideration, consideration	11,71,72,184
Coherent	11	consignment number	15
collapse	17	Constructive	11
Collect B/L	104	Constructive Total Loss	106
Commercial Invoice	104,105	Consular Invoice	105
commission	98,99	contact	27,82,88,89,115
Committee	153	Contract, contract	77,82,98,99,100
Communication Purpose	147	convenience	91,122,123,124
commodity	15	Conversational	11
Commodity Name	61	Convincing	11
compensation	120,122,123	copy	71,108
complain	15	cordial	127
complaint	19,20,120	Cordially	46,47
Complete	11	corporation	65
Completeness	11	Correct	11
Complimentary Close	46,47,54,55,56,57,139,146	Correctness	11
compromise	121	Correspondent Bank	112
Complimentary Closes	47	Cost and Freight	106
concern	76	Cost, Insurance and Freight	107,123
concerning	82	Counter Offer	83,85
conciliation	121	Courtesy, courtesy	11,130
Concise	11	cover	108,145
Conciseness	11	cover sheet	133,134,135
Conclusion	145,147	credit	63,64
Concrete	11	credit account	114,115,116,117
Concreteness	11	credit bureau	114,115
conditions	62,72,73,87	credit card	144
confident	79,171,173,178	credit grantor	114,115
confidential	174	Credit Information Reports	145
confirm	96,97	credit record	138
confirmation	77,78,80,108,118	currency	79,80
Confirmation of Order	83,119	Curriculum Vitae	182,183,184
Confirmed L/C	112,113	customer	97
Congratulation, congratulation	187,188	customs clearance	104,116,117
considerable	28	customs formality	103
considerate	18	Customs Invoice	105

【D】

D/A	104,111
D/P	104,111
damage	16,17,27,122,123
damaged goods	120
DANGER	121
Date, date	36,54,57,101
Date of Shipment	95
dealer	88,89
Dear	41,42,43,47
Dear Madam or Sir	42
Dear Sir/Ms	42
Dear Sirs	42,66
death	189
deduct	116,117
defeat	158
deferred payment	112
delay	101,102,103,116,117,140
delay in delivery	100
delay in Voyage	100
delayed shipment	100,120
delight	14,178
delinquent	166
Delivery, delivery	20,67,68,74,95,96,103,123,124
Delivery Date	61,95
demand	166
depreciation	68
Description, description	61,80,81,95,96
Descriptive Report	145
destination	110,135,136
different quality	120
different shipment	120
discolore	16
discount	72,73,92
discover	22
discrepancy	123,124
dispatch	73
distribute	156
distribution	64,65,160
Distributor, distributor	62,63,64,74,75,86,91,93
distributorship	88
dockworker	103
Documentary Bill	111
Documentary Bill of Exchange	111,112
Documentary Draft	104,111
Documentary Letter of Credit; Documentary Credit	112
Documents against Acceptance;	111
Documents against Payment	111
dope	162
Draft, draft	82,104,112
due	114,115
duplicate	92,94

【E】

E-mail, e-mail	11,12,46,51,56,138,143,144
email	138
E/L	117
Education	185
effective	115
electronic mail	138
embarrassing	18
Emoticon	141
Enc	35,52
Encl	52,65
Enclose, enclose	14,21,71,72,73,74,91,92,93,95,98,99,107,108,109114,118,183
Enclosure, enclosure	51,92
end	18
Envelope	58

equipment	62,63,96
establish	15,97
esteemed	126
Evaluation Report	145
evidence	147
Ex Factory	106
Ex Godown	106
Ex Warehouse	106
Examination Report	145
exclusive	101,102
exclusive distributorship agreement	87
exclusive selling agent	86
excuse	169
expect	20,21
expedite	96
expire	13,15
expiry	109
Export License	117
export matter	93
export sales agent	86
export terms	62
expressway	17

【F】

FA	103
facsimile	134
fail	15,19
faint praise	162
Faithfully	46
Family Name	41
far	141
FAS	106
fascinate	166
fat	166
favor	13
fax	85,96 97,101,102,108,109,134,136,137
feasibility	28
feel	76
financial standing	62,63
Findings	147
firm	65,74,78,84,130
Firm Offer	77
firm order	74,75
First Name	41
FOB	79,80,98,99,104,105,106,107
FOB Airport	106
for and against	156
force majeure	100,108,109,121
foreign selling agent	86
Formal Report	145
Format	54
forward	29,62,63,68,73 85,90,92,94,101102,128,131 132,134,138,143,144,184,185
Foul B/L	105
fraud	166
Free Alongside Ship	106
free delivery	74,75
freedom	166
Free Offer	77
Free On Board	106
Freight	95
freight charge	116,117
Freight / Carriage and Carriage Paid to	107
Freight / Carriage and Insurance Paid to	107
fulfill	76
Full Block Style	54,56,57
FWIW	141
FYI	80,141

【G】

General Average	106

Gentlemen	42	improve	26
glad	14,89	Inc	65
glad to	12,14	inconsistent	18
go along	167	inconvenience	102,137
graduate	178,182,183,184	incorporate	71
greeting	171	increase	18
guarantee	27,173	Indented Style	54,55,57
		inferior quality	120

【H】

		influx	101,102
had better	28,29	Informal Report	145
hand	141	information	79,80,87,88,92,95,96
happy	13,14,15	information Report	145
he/she	29	initial order	94
head office;	126	Inquiry, inquiry	61,66
Heading	136,138,145,146,155	70,74,75,80,81,101,102,129,135	
Health Certificate	105	Inside	57
hello	130	Inside Address	36,41,49,54,55,57
help	27	Inspection Certificate	105
helpful	164	install	16
hereby	122,123	Institute Cargo Clauses	106
herewith	125	insult	168
hesitate	172	Insurance, insurance	
hesitation	176,177,178		62,95,104,109,117
highway	17,18	Insurance Policy	105,109
home office	125,126	International Standard Book Number	
hospitality	128,188		98
house number	37	introduce	15
hot	168	Introduction	145
however	24,25	investigation	31,147
humble	141	investment	18
		Invoice, invoice	104,109,
		116,117,118,121,123,124	

【I】

I/L 117		IOW	141
ICC (Air)	106	Irrevocable	113
IMHO	141	Irrevocable L/C	96,97,112
IMO	141	ISBN	97,98
Identification Marks	51	issue	62,71,85,162,170
illegal shipment	120		
Import License	117		

[J]

job	185
Jp	82

[K]

Kindest regards	46
kindness	166

[L]

L/C	79,80,94,107,108,109,112 113,118
Ladies and Gentlemen	42,50
lane	17
latest	103
laugh	141
lead	17
leaflet	87,88
learn	29
least	19
lend	14
less	19
Letter of Credit	92,94,112
Letter of Recommendation	43,174
Letter of Reference, letter of reference	174,175,177,178
Letter Paper	33
Letterhead	33,34,47,49,57
like	26
line	17,64,65,88,93
list price	92,94
listen to me	165
literature	64,65,87,88,91,93
load	28
LOL	141
Long Report	31,145
longshoreman	103
Ltd	65

[M]

M.	42
M/R	111
M/S, M.S., m/s, m.s.	107,108
M/V, m/v, m.v.	108
mad	164
Mail Address	58
Mail Direction	58
mail remittance	112
main office	126
maker	17
manual	68,69,76
manufacture	64,72,94,101,103
manufacturer	17,81
Marine Insurance Policy	104
Marine Loss	106
market claim	120
Market Report	145
Marking	95
marriage	187
mate's receipt	111
maximum	19
may	26,27,72,88
maybe	29,164
meeting	152,154,155,156,158,159,160
Memorandum	145,146
merchandise	13
Messrs.	43
might	26,27
minutes	22,52
	151,152,154,155,156,157,161
mistake	163,164
Mixed-Punctuation Pattern	57
Mmes.	43
Mode of Packing	62
monetary units	195
money order	114,115

moralizing	162
more	19
most	19
motion	152,156,157,158
motorcar	17
motorway	17
Mr. or Ms.	42
Mses.	43
must	15,27,29

【N】

Negative Example	149
neglect	19,20
negligent	166
negotiable	105
negotiation	161,163
net	92
nice	18
No	165
non-delivery	120
non-shipment	120
nonnegotiable	109,110
note	96
Notice of Shipment	104
Notifying Bank	112
number of votes	156

【O】

oblige	12
objective	180
obstacles	166
obstinate	166
ocean freight	118,119
Offer, offer	14,70
	75,77,78,79,80,81,83,84,85,92
Offer on approval	77,78
Offer on sale or return	77
office	131,132,149,150,179
office director	131,132

One Topic in One Paragraph	32,45
Open-Punctuation Pattern	57
Opening Bank; Issuing Bank ;	
Establishing Bank	112
opinion	141
opportunity	15,131,132
or	19
Order,order	12,16,20,21,26
	29,79,92,93,94,95,96,98,101,102
	107,108,109,115,118,119,126,154
Order B/L	105
order form	72
Order Sheet	92
OTOH	141
ought to	162
overtax	101,102

【P】

P.O. Sheet	95
p.s.	53
Pack	80
Packing, packing	80,95
Packing List	105,109
Parcel Post Receipt	105
Partial Loss	106
Particular Average	106
pass	17,189
path	17
patronage	74,75
Payment, payment	81,82,92
	94,95,97,98,111,114,138,144
Payment in Advance	112
Per, per	48,102,108
perhaps	29
Permit	117
perfect	167
persevering	166
Personal Data	185

Personal History	182,184
Photo Only	58
place	12
PL	120
PLC	65
please	12,13,14,16,18,26,27,29 62,64,65,67,68,70,71,79,80,84,85 88,89,90,92,95,96,97,98,103,108 109,125,126,127,130,136,137 144,171,172,178114,115,116,117 118,119
pleasure	12,178,180,181
P.O.Sheet	95
position	184,185
possible	18
postgraduate	178,179,180,181
post postscript	53
Postal Code	39
postal order	115
Postscript	53
PPS	53,65
prefer	20
premium	105
Prepaid B/L	104
presentation	161,172,180
Presiding	155
pretty	166
Price, price	16,61,81,95,96
price list	94
principal	86
Printed Matter	58
prior sale	78,81,82
problem/solution	162
procedure	116,117
producer	17
products liability	120
Proforma Invoice	116,117
Progress Report	145
promise	20
prompt	18
propose	159
proposition	86
prosperous	128
PS	35,65
p.s.	53
Public Limited Company	65
Punctuation	57
Purchase Note	83
Purchase Order Sheet	95
purpose	28,139,147

[Q]

Q'ty, q'ty	96,97,123,124
Qualifications	186
quality	22,70,72,73,85,173
Quantity, quantity	61,79,80,95,97,123,124
query	88,89
quote	16

[R]

rain	16
range	87,88
Re, re	51,143
recall	102
receive	17
Received B/L	105
recommend	81,82,149,150,151,157,158,159 162,175,176,177,178,179,180,181
Recommendation, recommendation	147,150,157
Recommendation Report	145
reconsider	14
Ref	34,49
ref.	118,119
Reference, reference	

	101,102,103,186
Reference Number	49
refuse	167
regard	75,76,82
Registered	58
regret	13,14,15,19,76,101,102
Regular Meeting	154
regular order	21
reliability	73
remittance	111
rental grade	125,126
reply	64,70,74,79,80,83,85,88,91
	93,95,96,101,138,140,143,144
report	31,147,149,156
representation	87,88
representative samples	88
represent	88,89
Request, request	13,14,19,67,71,72
	75,76,81,88,90,157,170,174,186
Research Paper	31
resolution	152,156
Respectfully, respectfully	46,47
respectfully submitted	160
response	62,81,82,183,184
responsibility	24,149
responsible	150,151,184,185
RESUME, Resume, resume	
	182,183,184,185
retail stores	63
return	28,64
Return Address	44,58
return airmail	90,98,99
retail	148
retrieval	149
retrieve	150,151
review	114,115,150
Revise	150
Revocable L/C	112,113

road	17
roadway	17
Room	37
route	17

【S】

s/he	29
s/s	108
sale	77
Sale Note	83
Sales Contract	95
Sales Note	95
Salutation	41,42,46,47,49,50,54,56
	57,66,134,139,146,174,177,190
Sanitary Certificate	105
satisfactory	167
schedule	101
scrawny	166
Sea Mail	58
second	157
Self-introduction sheet	184
selling agent	86
Selling Offer	77
Semiblock Style	54,55,57
send	16,17
settlement	116,117
sexist	42
sexual harassment	29
shall	26,28
ship	13
	19,26,101,103,108,109,110,118
Shipment, shipment	18,79,81
	92,94,96,98,100,107,108,
	109,116,117,118,123,124
Shipped B/L	105
Shipping Advice	104,110
Shipping Documents	104,112
Shipping Parcel Receipt	105

shortage	120
Short Report	31,145
should	27
sight	82
Signature	47,51,54
Signature Line	55,57
significantly	18
Simplified Style	54,56
Sincerely,	46,47,48,128
slender	166
Smiley	141
Softener, softener	13,14,68
71,80,89,96,119,165,166,174,178	
sole agent	86
soon	18
sorry	14,15,165
spare	169
Special Delivery	58
Special Talent	182
specification	148
specify	20
SS	102
standing	63,64
Standing Committee	154
stock	20,126
Straight B/L	105
street	17
Street Designators	40
strike	103,108
study	31
Subject, subject	31,32,35
50,51,66,77,78,80,81,82,89,139	
Subject Line	50
submit	22
subscription	144
successful	166
suggest	159
suggestion	20,26,27,158
suit	121
sum up	169
Supplementary Matter	145
sure	167
Surface	58
surface mail	97,98
sympathize	186,189

【T】

Table of Contents	145
Tag question	166
tax-exemption	74,75
Technical Purpose	147
tell	16
tentative	108
temper	168
term	72,73,81,82,87,92,95,96
terms and conditions	63
Terms of Payment	62
Test Report	149,150,151
thank	27
therefore	24,25
therein	123
thoughtful	188
threatening	162
thoroughfare	17
TIA	141
Time of Shipment	61
Title Page	145
To Whom It May Concern:	43,174,177
toll road	17
Tone, tone	12,14
Topic	139
Total Loss, total loss	106,122,123
touchy	168
track	17
trade-ins	74,75

transfer	131,132
Transferable L/C	112,113
Transport Document	111
trial	95,96
triplicate	98,99
truly	46,47
trust	93,94,97,98,101,109,110,166
turn down	15
turnover	87,88

【U】

unavailable	76
Unconfirmed L/C	113
understand	169
unit	80,96,97
unpack	22
update	138
use	16

【V】

Valentine Day	194
validity	77,108,109,118,119
value	118,123,124
variety	15
Vitae	182,184
void	27

【W】

want	26,27
Warmest regards	46
WARNING	121
warranty	13,15,92,94
way	141
well-liked	18
well-respected	18
whereby	91,93
wholesale price list	125,126
will	88, 26,27,28
wish	12,13
with	85,88
word	141
would	27,28
Work Experience	182
worth	141
wrong article	120

【Y】

yell	164
yes	164
you	163,164

【Z】

ZIP	39
zone improvement plan	39

著者略歴　篠田義明（しのだ・よしあき）

現在　早稲田大学商学部教授、教育学部／理工学部大学院兼任教授　日本実用英語学会会長
商業英語検定（日本商工会議所主催）専門委員、TEP Test（早稲田大学・ミシガン大学実用ライティング英語検定試験）検定委員長、1995年にミシガン州アナーバー市より名誉市民の称号を受ける。
　官公庁（参議院や郵政省など）や数多くの企業でも Technical Communication in English, Business Communication in English,『ロジカル・ドキュメント作成法』（日本文）,『分かり易い文章の書き方』（日本文）などを指導中。

著者：『テクニカル・イングリッシュ論理と展開』,『科学技術英語の正しい訳し方』,『科学技術英文の書き方セミナー』,『科学技術英文の実例と書き方』,『英語感覚が身につく本』ほか（南雲堂）。
　　　『工業英語の語法』,『社会で役立つ英語習得のテクニック』ほか（研究社出版）。
　　　『英語の落とし穴』,『実務英語 Q & A』（大修館書店）。
　　　『コミュニケーション技術』（中公新書）,『通じる文章の技術』（ごま書房）
　　　『技術英語の常識』（ジャパンタイムズ社）
　　　『使える英語が見えてくる』（洋販出版）
　　　『国際会議・スピーチに必要な英語表現』,『ネゴシエーション・会議に必要な英語表現』,『パーティ・プレゼンテーションに必要な英語表現』（日興企画）ほか。

IT時代のオールラウンド　ビジネス英語		[1-390]
Business Communication for All Purposes in the IT Age		
1　刷　2001年6月15日		
著　者	篠田　義明	Yoshiaki Shinoda
発行者	南雲　一範	Kazunori Nagumo
発行所	株式会社　南雲堂	
	〒162-0801　東京都新宿区山吹町361	
	NAN'UN-DO Publishing Co., Ltd.	
	361 Yamabuki-cho, Shinjuku-ku, Tokyo 162-0801, Japan	
	振替口座：00160-0-46863	
	TEL: 03-3268-2311（代表）／FAX: 03-3269-2486	
	編集者　TA／RY	
製版所	URO Project	
装　丁	岡田デザイン事務所	
検　印	省　略	
コード	ISBN 4-523-26390-6　C0082	
		Printed in Japan

E-mail　nanundo@post.email.ne.jp
Home-page　http://www.mmjp.or.jp/nanun-do